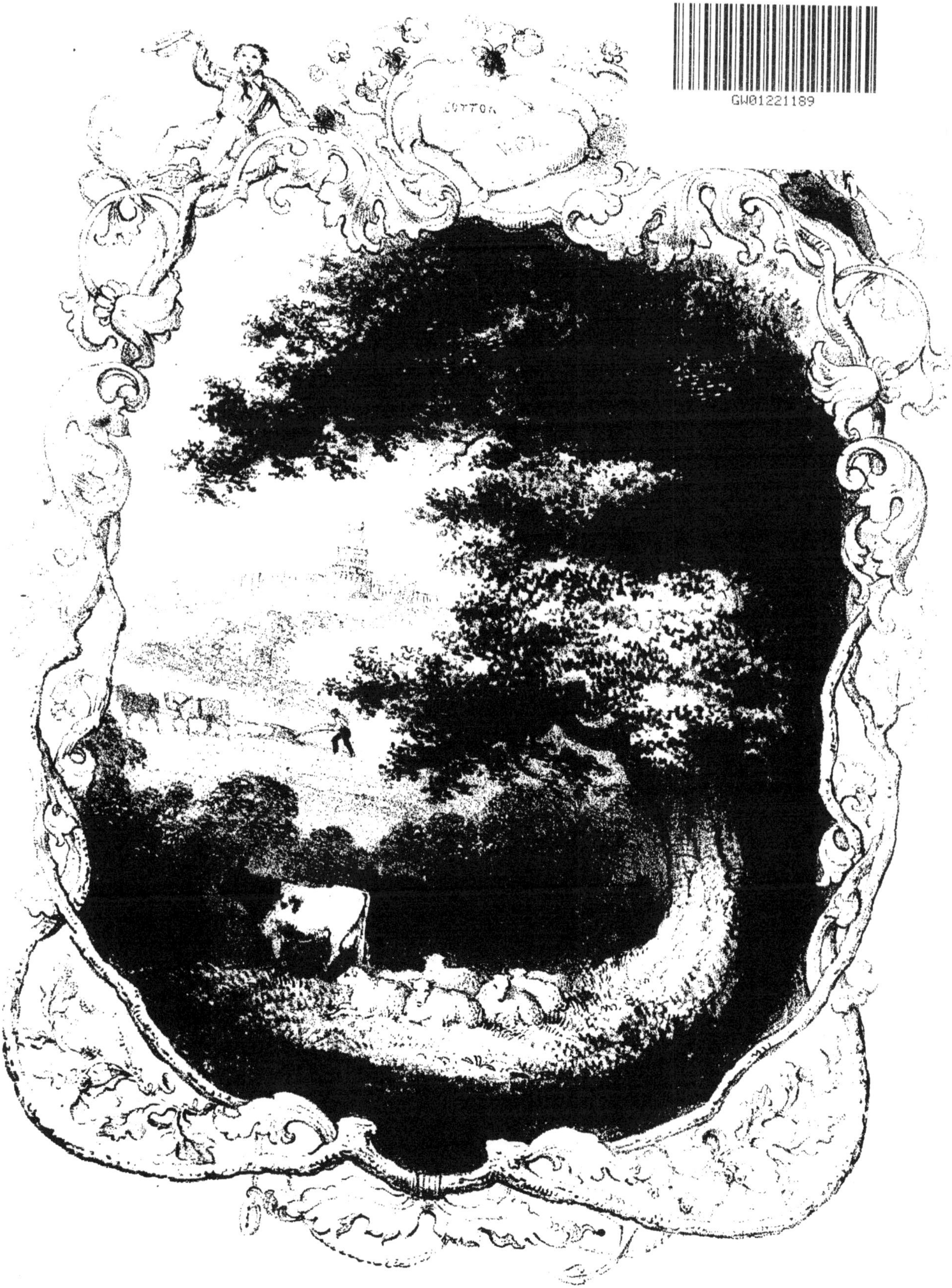

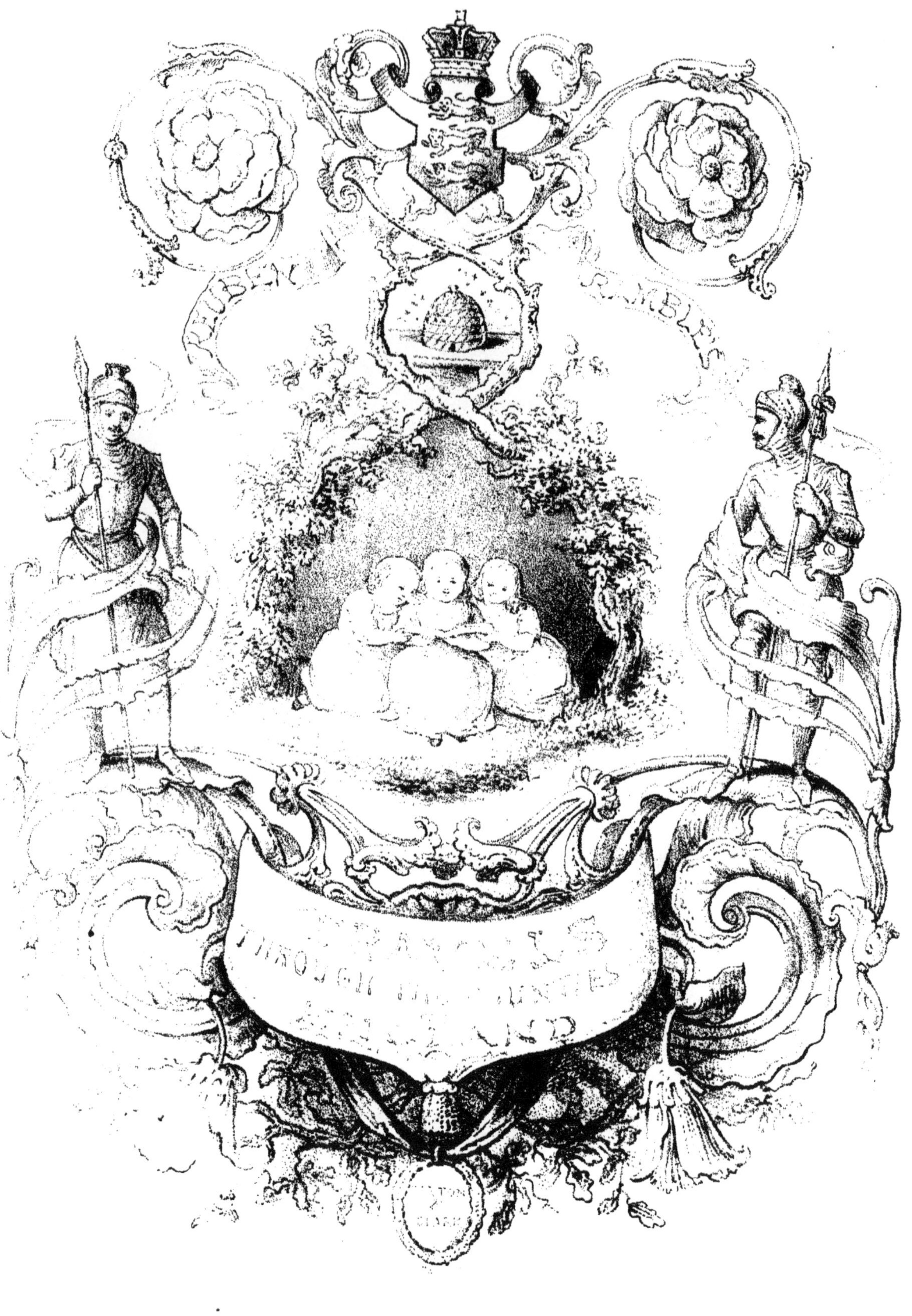
THROUGH

REUBEN RAMBLE'S

TRAVELS

THROUGH

THE COUNTIES OF ENGLAND.

With Maps and Historical Vignettes.

BOOK, PRINT, AND   MAP PUBLISHERS.

DARTON AND CLARK, 58 HOLBORN HILL

PREFACE.

In presenting to the Public this Juvenile Introduction to the English Counties, it may be remarked, that though there are excellent atlases and class books on general geography in abundance, still there is not a single work, calculated by its embellishments and simplicity of style, to lure the youthful multitude into that most interesting and important of all studies—*the geographical knowledge of their native land.*

In this Work the Author has given, in Forty Maps, the whole of the English Counties; each County being separately brought under notice to convey an accurate notion of its form and general outline, with a scale by which the little geographer may ascertain the superficial extent and the distance from one place to another.

In addition to the Maps, numerous Vignette Views are also given of the various topographical peculiarities and historical events, which will tend more effectually to fix the Counties on the recollection.

In the letter-press portion of the work the Author has endeavoured to attain comprehensiveness and brevity; a difficult task—but one which he hopes he has successfully accomplished. He has given the superficial extent—the population—the chief town—the peculiarity of position, if any, in regard to the whole island—and the nature of the soil, the produce of the county, and the historical records.

With the assistance of a parent, or elder brother or sister, it is hoped the Work may be not only extensively useful, but highly interesting; and, with such hope, it is now respectfully committed to the public attention.

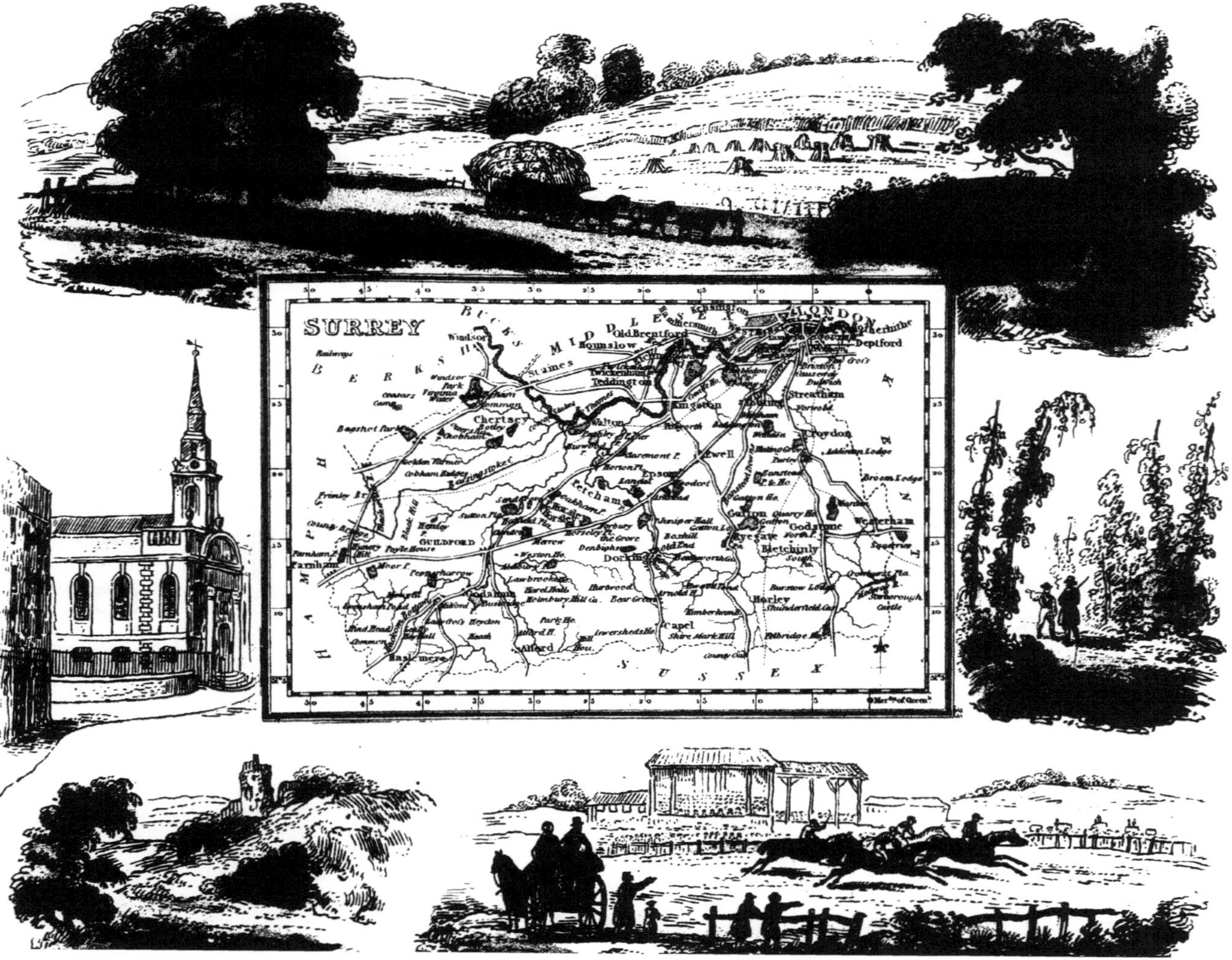

SURREY.

Surrey is rather larger than Middlesex, and contains 580,000 people; 317,000 of whom are in Southwark, which is a part of London. Surrey is a beautiful county, and is overspread with woods and streams and gently rising hills. It contains a great many fine estates and beautiful houses. There is a long and high hill, called the Hog's Back, which lies between the towns of Farnham and Guildford; and from the top of this hill there are most beautiful views on both sides. I do not know any spot from which you may see more beautiful English scenery than here. The beauty of English scenery is not so much in great and wonderful natural objects, such as mountains, and cliffs and lakes, water-falls and rivers; but an English landscape presents a surface of country, varied with low hills and vallies, richly cultivated with corn-fields, and fine timber trees, handsome houses in the midst of parks and lawns, with comfortable-looking cottages for the poor. This is what you may see in Surrey.

The produce of the county consists chiefly of corn, hay, and hops. The hops are grown near Farnham, and are of excellent quality. They make the neighbourhood look very pretty in the Autumn, when they are full grown. The grounds in which they grow are called hop-gardens, and I will tell you how they are cultivated. The young plants are raised from seed or from young shoots, which readily take root. They are planted in rows, six feet a-part, and as they grow up, they twine round high poles stuck in the ground. When a plant has reached the top of its pole it often stretches across to the next pole, and twines round it; and as the hops become ripe, you see them hanging from the branches in beautiful festoons. In the month of September, the hop-plant is cut off near the ground, the pole is taken down, and men, women, and children are employed in great numbers in picking off the hops which are then dried and packed into large bags called pockets.

At Farnham there is an ancient castle, where the Bishop of Winchester now lives. At a short distance from the town, there are the ruins of the famous Abbey of Waverley.

Epsom is one of the most famous places in the kingdom for horse-racing.

At Esher, Cardinal Wolsey, who was a great man in the time of Henry VIII., had an estate, and there is still remaining a tower, which you may see in the picture, called Wolsey's Tower.

There are two railways through Surrey; one the South-Western, which goes on to Southampton; and the other goes through Croydon to Brighton.

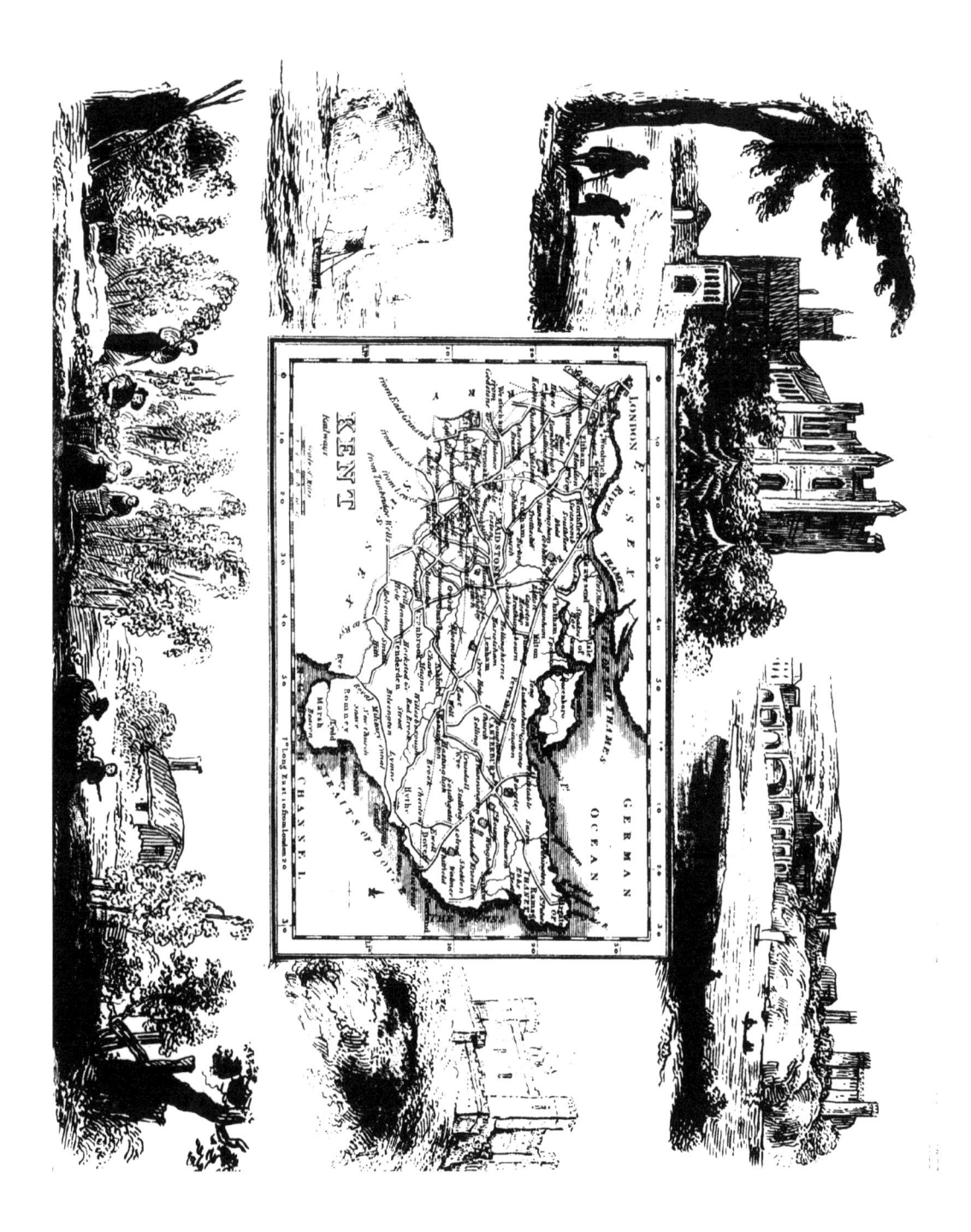

KENT

KENT.

The county of Kent is sixty miles long, and forty miles wide. It is bounded on the North side by the river Thames and the German Ocean, and on the East by the Straits of Dover; and is nearer to the coast of France than any other part of England. It contains 548,000 inhabitants. There are several islands belonging to Kent, the most remarkable of which is the Isle of Thanet. I shall presently mention this island to you again. It is now separated from the main land by a very narrow stream, but it was formerly divided by a considerable channel.

Some parts of Kent are very beautiful. Its chief produce consists of hops, filberts, fruit of various kinds and vegetables, which are sent to London in large quantities. The hop-grounds look very beautiful when the hops are ripe, and the season of gathering them is a very pleasant time. You will find something said of the growth of hops in the account of Surrey.

There are two cities in Kent—Canterbury and Rochester. Canterbury is a famous place, for the Arch-Bishop of Canterbury is the Primate of all England; and it is the place where Augustine first founded a Church, when he was sent over to convert the Saxons by the Bishop of Rome, in the year 596. The

KENT.

Saxons had overcome the Britons, and driven out the British clergy, and were living as heathens; and the Bishop of Rome, learning this, thought it right to send a missionary to convert them. Rochester, like Canterbury, is a very ancient place, but it is not nearly such a pleasant one. It stands on one side of a river, and is united with the town of Stroud, which is on the other side, by a bridge.

Dover is a very interesting place, and has a very old castle. Close by the town is the cliff, called Shakspere's Cliff, which has become so celebrated from its being described in Shakspere's play of "King Lear." There is a railway from Dover to London, which runs quite through the county of Kent.

When Julius Cæsar first came to England, fifty-two years before the birth of Christ, he landed on the coast of Kent, between Dover and Deal. Nearly five hundred years afterwards, the British King, Vortigern, having invited over the Saxons to help him against his enemies, gave them the Isle of Thanet to dwell in. But they did not long remain satisfied with such narrow limits, but took possession of the whole county, and set up the kingdom of Kent, which was one of the states of the Saxon Heptarchy. Ethelbert was King here when Augustine came to convert the Saxons, as I have told you above.

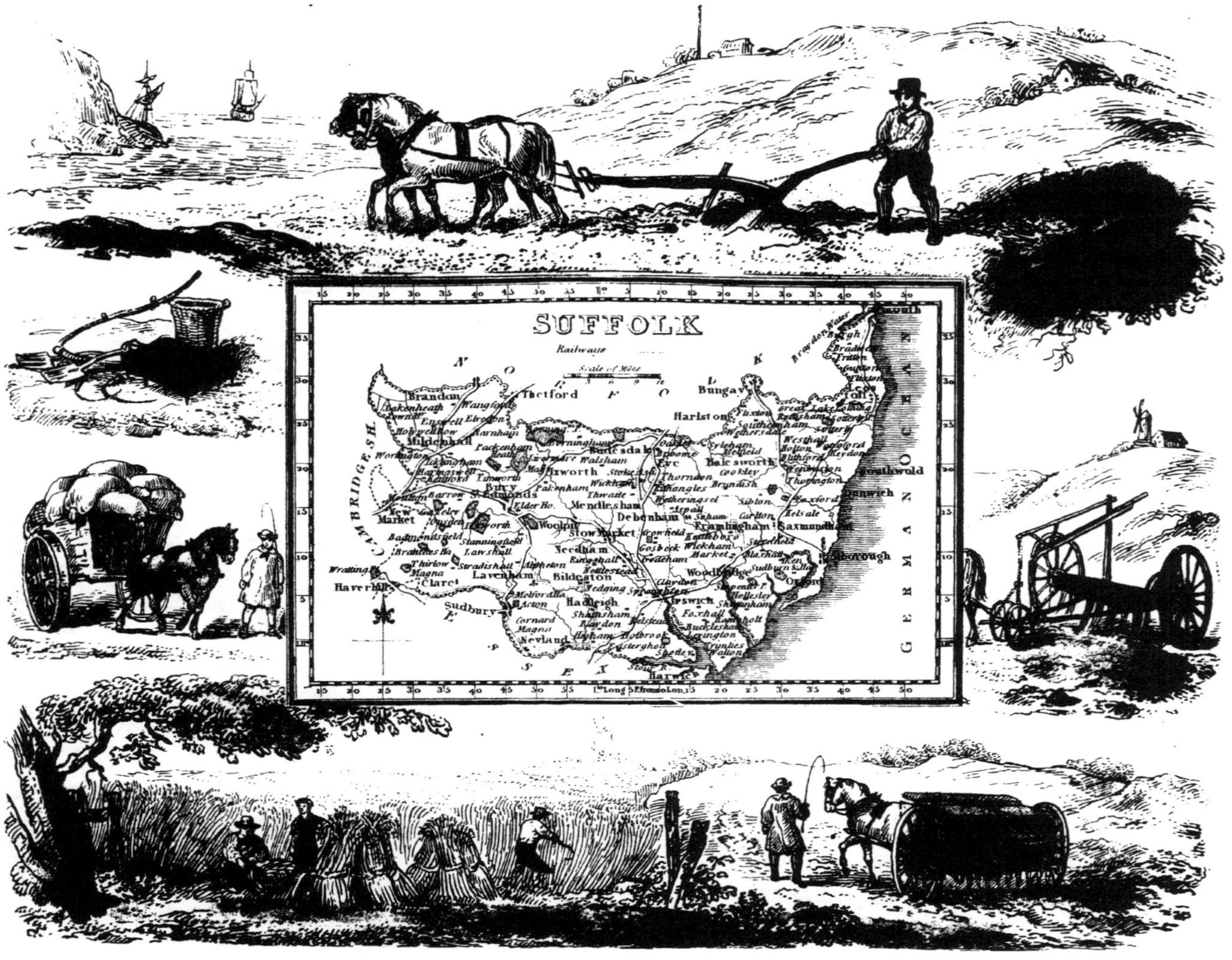
SUFFOLK
Railways
Scale of Miles
NORFOLK
CAMBRIDGE SH.
GERMAN OCEAN
ESSEX
Brandon
Thetford
Bungay
Harleston
Mildenhall
Bury St. Edmunds
Ixworth
Eye
Halesworth
Southwold
Dunwich
Newmarket
Mendlesham
Debenham
Framlingham
Saxmundham
Stow Market
Needham
Woodbridge
Orford
Aldborough
Lavenham
Bildeston
Hadleigh
Ipswich
Haverhill
Clare
Sudbury
Harwich
Long. E. from London

SUFFOLK.

Suffolk is bounded on the East side by the German ocean. Its length is sixty-eight miles, and its breadth fifty-two miles. It contains 315,000 people. The Eastern Counties Railway, which runs from London to Yarmouth, in Norfolk, passes through Suffolk. It contains two county-towns, Ipswich and Bury St. Edmunds.

Suffolk is a famous county for farmers and for every thing connected with agriculture. The ploughs and other farming implements made at Ipswich, by Ransoms, are celebrated all over England. The single-hand plough, which you may see in the picture, is almost peculiar to this county. Many of the farmers are rich, and take great delight in having all their farm buildings and instruments of husbandry very complete. Steam engines are sometimes used here for ploughing and other purposes. It is one of the best cultivated spots in England, and its chief produce is corn. The Suffolk pigs and cart horses, or Suffolk cobs, as they are often called, are of great excellence.

The name of Suffolk comes from the two words "South" and "Folk." When a party of the Saxons settled in this part of England, they were divided into two bodies, the North Folk and the South Folk;

SUFFOLK.

and from these the counties of Norfolk and Suffolk had their names. The two were united in the kingdom of East Anglia. When Ethelred, the brother of Alfred the Great, ruled over England, Edmund was king of this part under him. The Danes made an attack on the coast, and took King Edmund prisoner. They promised him life and liberty, if he would renounce his faith in Christ, and become a heathen. He refused, and they murdered him on the spot. His body was afterwards removed to Bury St. Edmund's, or St. Edmund's Bury, which took its name from this circumstance. There are the ruins of an old Abbey in this place, which are very well worth looking at. There are also some interesting remains of Abbeys—of Sibton Abbey, near Yoxford; Butley Abbey, near Woodbridge; and of several others; for there seems to have been a great number of convents and monasteries in this county in former days.

Ipswich is an ancient town, and is remarkable for its never having been much injured by fire or war. In consequence of this the houses stand in the same situations as they used to do in very ancient times, and the streets are narrow and irregular. Cardinal Wolsey established a grammar school here, which he intended should be preparatory to Christ Church College, Oxford, of which he was the founder.

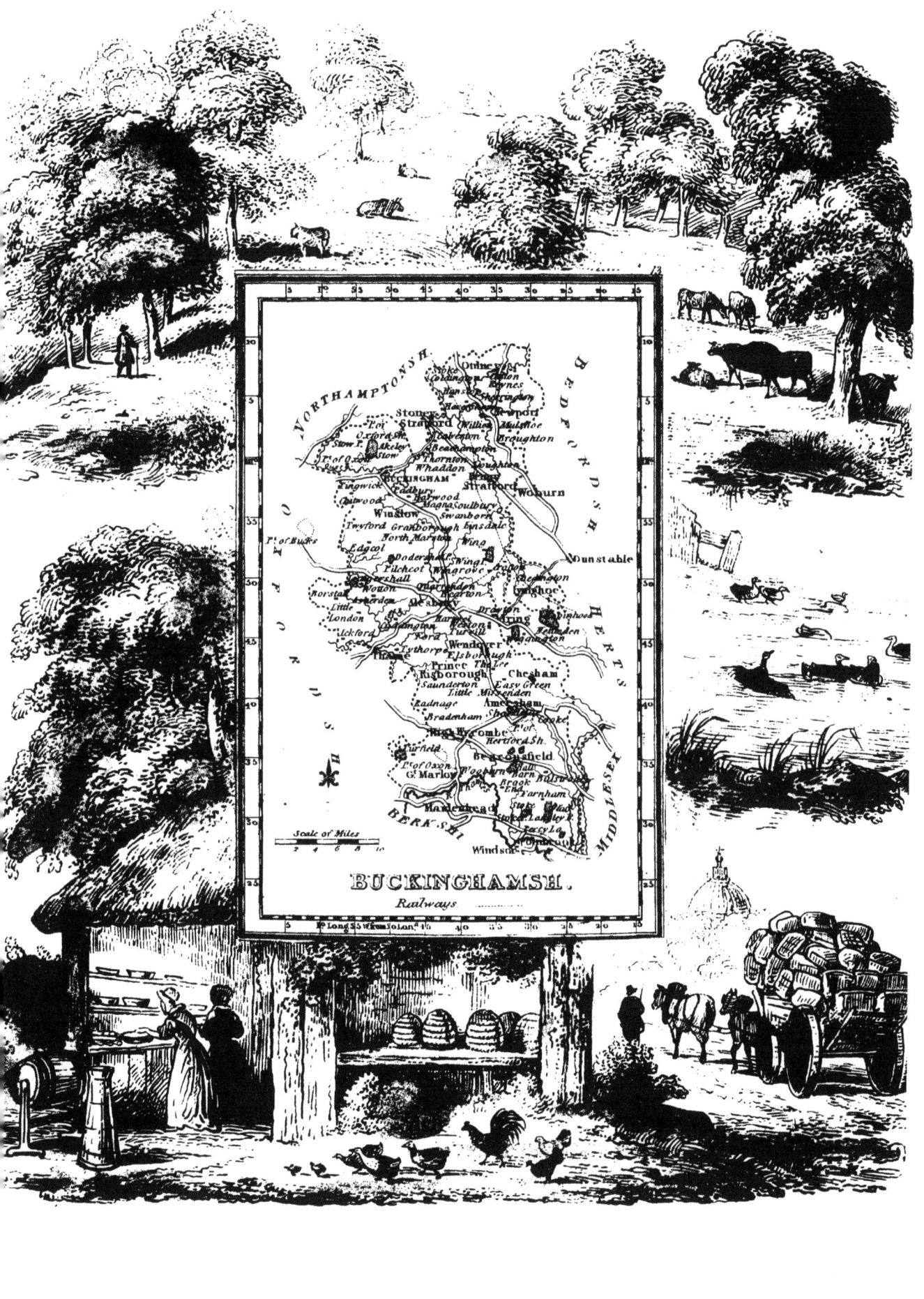

BUCKINGHAMSH.
Railways

BUCKINGHAMSHIRE.

This county is fifty-three miles in length, and about twenty miles in width. The county-town is Aylesbury and not the town of Buckingham, although it bears the same name as the county. The whole county contains about 160,000 people. You may see in the map that no part of it touches the sea.

There are a great many beech trees in Buckinghamshire, and some people have thought that the name was originally Beech-inghamshire from this circumstance. The beech trees grow upon and near a range of chalk hills, called the Chiltern Hills. The beech timber is made into chairs, wood bowls, and other articles of the kind, which are carried to London and to distant parts of the country.

A great part of the county has a very rich soil, about half of which is in pasture land, and the other half cultivated for corn. The farmers keep a great many cows, and make a large quantity of butter, which is made up into rolls weighing two pounds each, and packed in nearly square baskets, called Flats, that are sent to London. A great deal of the butter that is eaten in London comes out of Buckinghamshire. It is conveyed sometimes in waggons, but more frequently by the railways. There are two railways passing through the county,

BUCKINGHAMSHIRE.

the Great Western and the London and Birmingham.

Many calves and pigs are also sent to London from Buckinghamshire, and a vast quantity of ducks. The farmers have a way of getting fine ducks very early in the season. They hatch the duck-eggs under hens, and bring up the ducklings very carefully in the house. It is calculated that twenty thousand pounds' worth of ducks are sent every year from the whole county to London.

Near the town of Buckingham is Stowe, the estate of the Duke of Buckingham. The house was originally built in the reign of Queen Elizabeth, though it has been much altered and enlarged since. The grounds are very beautiful, and are adorned with temples, grottos, lakes and bridges. The poet Pope spent some time here, and has described the place in his poetry. This county seems to have been a favourite spot of poets; for at Stoke-Poges, near Maidenhead, Gray lived for some time; and it is supposed that his "Elegy in a Country Churchyard" refers to the churchyard of that place, where his body now lies buried. At Olney or Oulney, Cowper lived with his friend, the Rev. John Newton, who was the Vicar; and from this town the celebrated Olney Hymns took their name, some of them having been written by Cowper and some by Newton.

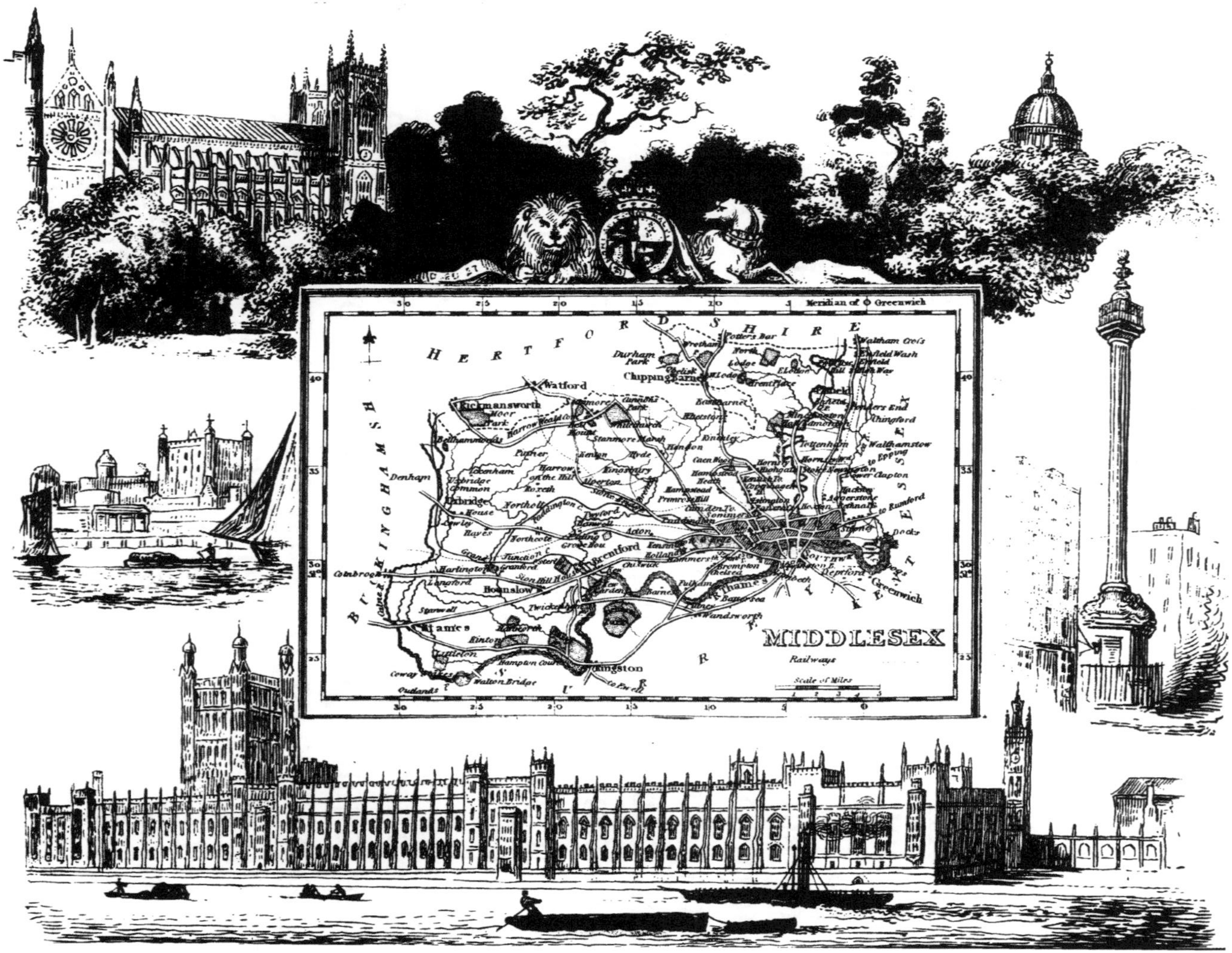

MIDDLESEX.

Middlesex is a very small county, but it contains a great many people. It is only 23 miles long, and 15 miles broad; but more than a million and a half of people live in it, and of these about 1,200,000 are in London. Middlesex is a fertile county, and contains a great deal of wood. The parts near London are very beautiful, full of rich gardens, fields, trees and good houses.

If you look in the map you will see that the river Thames runs along the South side of the county, and divides it from Surrey. A large part of London, which is called Southwark, is in Surrey, and contains 317,000 people; so that the whole of London has 1,517,000 inhabitants. The rest of London is joined to Southwark by six noble bridges over the river: London Bridge, Blackfriars, Waterloo and Westminster, which are built of stone; and Southwark and Vauxhall, which are of iron.

Large ships come up the river Thames nearly as far as London Bridge, and small steam boats and boats of all kinds are continually passing under the bridges, and some of them go up the river as far as Richmond.

It seems that London has been a great city for more than two thousand years, though we know but little of its early state. It was an ancient British town before the Romans came here under Julius Cæsar, but you may be sure it was very different then from what it is now. It was most likely nothing but some mud cottages, with a bank of earth thrown up round them. The Romans, when they lived in Britain, improved the city very much, as we know from the fine pavements of Roman workmanship which are sometimes found under the earth in many of the streets. It is said, that the part of the Tower of London called the White Tower was built by Julius Cæsar, but it is more likely that it was founded by William the Conqueror.

St. Paul's Cathedral and Westminster Abbey were first built more than twelve hundred years ago by Sebert, the Saxon King of Essex and Middlesex. They have both been rebuilt several times since then, and the present Westminster Abbey was raised partly in the reign of Edward I. and part in the reign of Henry VII.; and St. Paul's, of which Sir Christopher Wren was the architect, in the reign of James II.

In the year 1666, a great part of London was burned down, and the Monument near London Bridge was made to commemorate it.

The new Houses of Parliament, which are building near Westminster Bridge, will be, when they are finished, one of the very finest of the buildings of London.

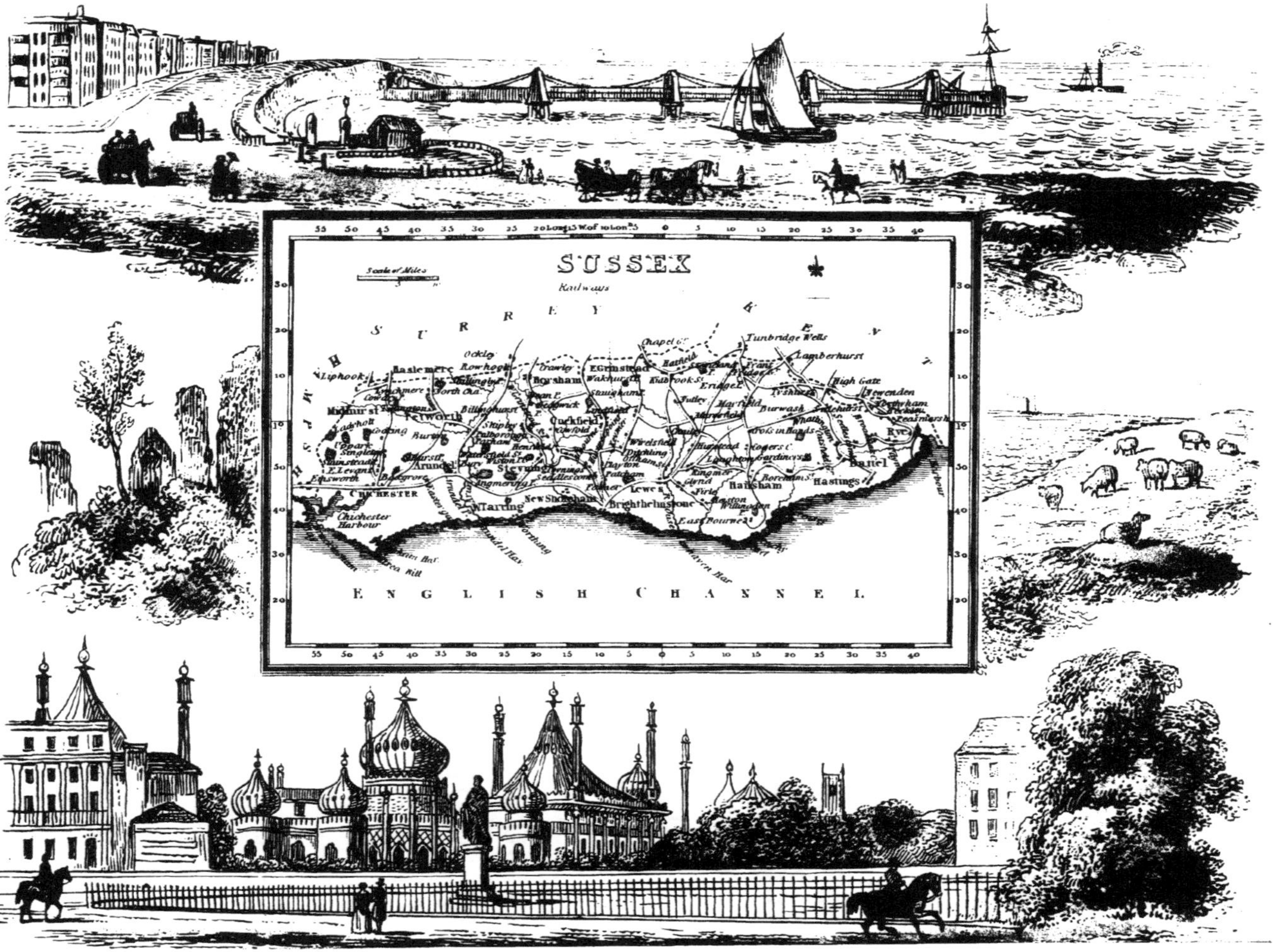
SUSSEX
Railways
Scale of Miles
SURREY
KENT
HAMPSH
ENGLISH CHANNEL
Tunbridge Wells
Lamberhurst
Liphook
Haslemere
Petworth
Horsham
Cuckfield
E.Grinstead
CHICHESTER
Chichester Harbour
Arundel
Steyning
New Shoreham
Brighthelmstone
Lewes
Hailsham
Battel
Hastings
Rye
East Bourne

SUSSEX.

This county is situated at the South-eastern corner of England, and is bounded on the South by the English Channel. It is seventy-six miles in length, and twenty in width. The population is nearly 300,000. The county-town is Lewes.

The Western part of Sussex is fertile, but in the Eastern part there is a long range of chalk hills, the surface of which is only good for feeding sheep. This tract is called the South Downs, and the sheep that live upon it are very excellent, though not large. The middle part of the county is called the Weald, and was once a forest. A great part of it is cultivated, but it is by no means fertile.

Sussex was once a kingdom, and was founded by Ella, the Saxon chief, in 477. The name comes from the South Saxons, respecting whom I have told you something in the account of Essex. King Alfred lived here for some time; and near a small place named Alfriston, there are the remains of a castle he built. But the most famous historical event that ever occurred in Sussex, was the landing of William the Norman Conqueror. You may read in the History of England how he laid claim to the throne, which Harold had taken possession of immediately after the death of Edward the Con-

SUSSEX.

fessor. Harold had collected a force to meet him, when news arrived that the Danes had landed in the North, and were ravaging the country. He accordingly marched his army northward as fast as he could, and gained a great victory over the Danes. In the mean time, William had landed his troops, and had taken up his position at Hastings. This was a bad thing for Harold, for if he had been on the spot, he probably might have destroyed a great part of the Norman army as they were landing, or before they had fortified a camp. He returned immediately after his victory, and fought a battle with William, where the town of Battle now stands. He was conquered, as you know, and it was generally believed that he was slain; but of this there is some doubt. William soon afterwards founded the Abbey of Battle, of which some part is still standing.

Chichester is a very ancient city, and contains a fine old cathedral. The city was founded by the Romans, and was a place of great importance in Saxon times.

Brighton is a large and fashionable place, where there is a very noble pier, constructed chiefly of iron bars and chains. Here is also a palace of very strange form, which was built by King George IV. This town was probably founded in very early times, but it was quite a small place till within the last sixty years.

ESSEX

ESSEX.

This county is about fifty miles from the East to the West side, and thirty-seven miles from North to South. One side of it is open to the German Ocean, and on the South it is bounded by the river Thames. It contains 345,000 inhabitants. The county town is Chelmsford, which has its name from the river Chelmer, which, in ancient times, used to be forded near this spot.

The land in Essex is generally flat, but in some parts it is very fertile, and produces great quantities of corn and hay. Many calves are also fatted here and sent to London. Most of the produce is now sent to London by the Eastern Counties Railway, which is marked in the map. On the coast, a great quantity of oysters are taken, which are called Colchester oysters, and are very much celebrated.

Colchester is a very pleasant and interesting place, being of great antiquity. It was most likely founded by the Romans, as were perhaps all the towns of which the names end with "chester," which comes from the latin word "castra," a camp. The word Colchester signifies a camp, or castle on the river Colne, which runs by the town. Colchester Castle is a very ancient building, and most likely some part of it was built by the Romans. There are some remains of a Roman road, which may now

ESSEX.

be traced running from Colchester to Bishop Stortford. A great many coins, urns, cups, buckles, tesselated pavements, and other articles of Roman workmanship, have also been found in the neighbourhood. Colchester was a city; that is, it had a Bishop and a Cathedral, as early as the year 314, while the Romans were still ruling in Britain.

When the Saxons had conquered England, Essex was a distinct kingdom, and then included Middlesex. The name Essex comes from the East Saxons, anp the name Middlesex from the Middle Saxons; for some of the Saxons who first came to England, separated into four great bodies; the other two of which were the South Saxons, who peopled Sussex, and the West Saxons, who formed what was then the kingdom of Wessex.

As the coast of Essex is opposite the coasts of Denmark and Norway, it was much exposed to the attacks of the Northmen or Danes, as they are often called; and it was here, and especially on Mersea Island, that the famous chief Hastings lived, and defied the power of King Alfred for some time, though at last he was driven out. Hastings was of a very savage and inhuman disposition. King Alfred once, having taken his wife and children prisoners, treated them kindly, and sent them home; but Hastings did not ever thank him for his generosity, and went on robbing and destroying as he had done before.

HERTFORDSHIRE

HERTFORDSHIRE.

The map will shew you that Hertfordshire is an inland county. It is thirty-nine miles long, and twenty-five miles wide. It contains 157,000 people. The county town is Hertford. The London and Birmingham railway runs through the county from Watford to Tring.

There are a great many orchards and vegetable gardens in Hertfordshire; and apples, cherries, potatoes, pease, and cabbages are sent to London in great quantities. Much barley is also grown here, which is made into malt. In the town of Hitchen, the trade in malt is carried on to a great extent.

The town of Hertford is very ancient, and was probably founded in the time of the old Britons. The castle, of which some ruins now remain, was built by Edward the elder, son of Alfred the Great. There is in Hertford a school connected with Christ's Hospital in London, where more than three hundred boys and eighty girls are educated. There is also a school for preparing boys for the College at Haileybury, about three miles from Hertford, where young men, intended for the service of the East India Company, are taught the Eastern languages.

St. Albans is also a very old place, and contains a fine Church, which is part of an ancient Abbey founded by Offa, the Saxon King of Mercia, in 793. It was named after St. Alban, who suffered martyr-

HERTFORDSHIRE.

dom in the reign of the Roman Emperor Dioclesian; and was the first man who laid down his life in this country for the sake of the Christian faith. He was converted from Paganism by a clergyman, to whom, when pursued by his persecutors, Alban gave shelter from kindness of heart. When he became a Christian, the Romans beheaded him along with a soldier, who had become a Christian through his teaching.

Close to St. Albans are a few ruins, which are the remains of the town of Verulam, which was the capital of the kingdom of Cassivelaunus, the British King, who was conquered by Julius Cæsar. It was here that the great Queen Boadicea gained a victory over the Romans, in the time of Claudius Cæsar. The place afterwards became a Roman station. The present town of St. Albans was founded fifty years before the Norman conquest, and from that time Verulam declined.

One of the great curiosities of Hertfordshire is Waltham Cross, which was built by the command of Edward I. in honour of Queen Eleanor, his virtuous and affectionate wife. She died in Lincolnshire; and as her body was brought to Westminster Abbey to be buried, wherever it remained a night, there the King had a cross built. On the place at which it stopped last before it reached the Abbey, there once stood Charing Cross, of which now only the name remains.

Dropping Well

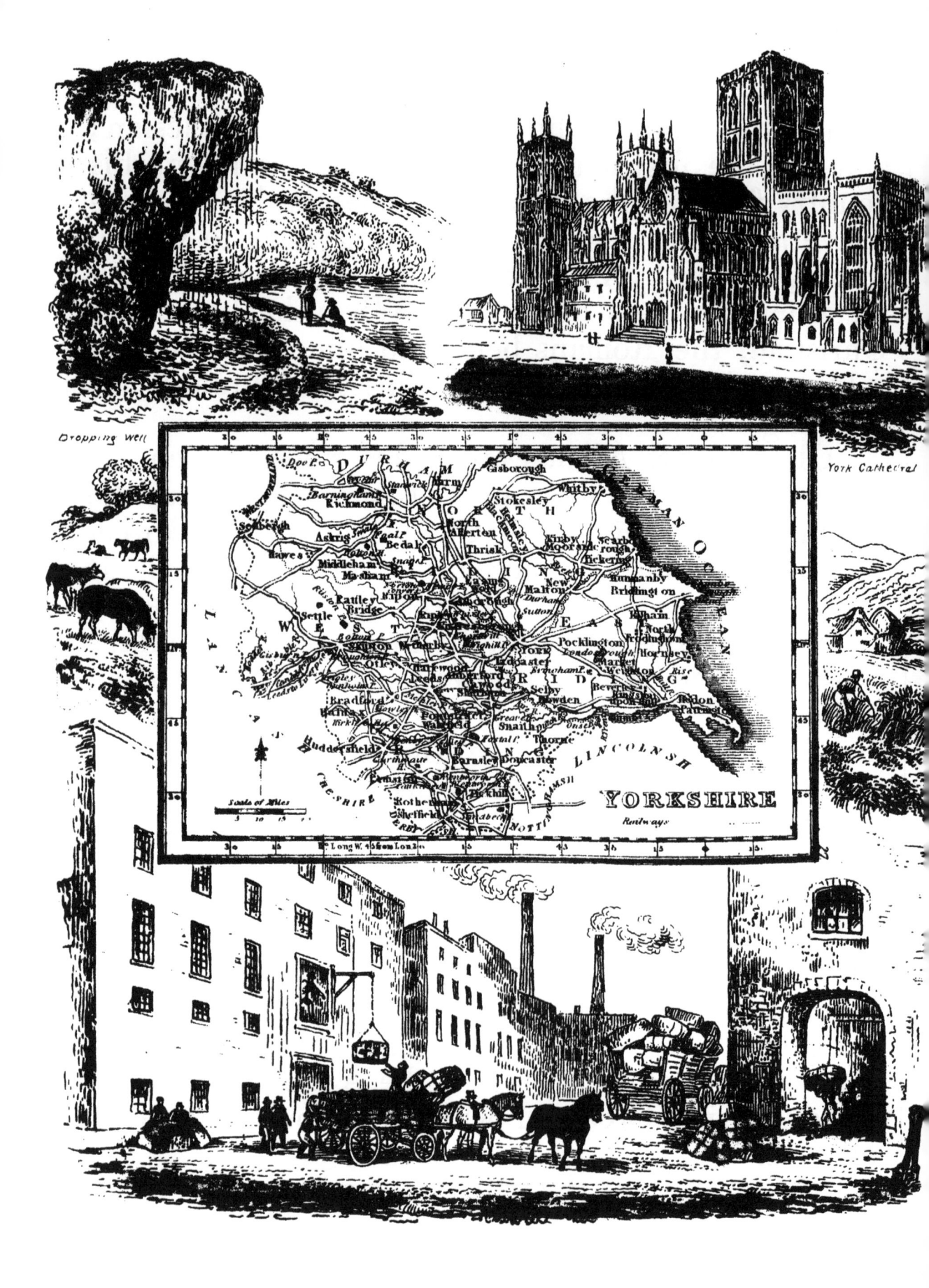

York Cathedral

YORKSHIRE

YORKSHIRE.

This is the largest of the English counties. It is eighty-seven miles from North to South, and one hundred from East to West. Its population is 1,591,000. It is divided into three parts, called Ridings, which are distinguished as the North, East and West Riding. These are almost like separate counties.

The WEST RIDING is by far the most populous. It contains more than a million of people. It produces coal, iron, lead and pipe-clay, in great abundance; and the soil in some parts is very fertile. Ripon, which is situated in this Riding, has lately become a city again. There was a Bishop of Ripon in very ancient times, but the see was moved to Durham. There was a very fine old church there, which is now used as a Cathedral. Near Ripon there is the ruin of an ancient Abbey, called Fountains Abbey, which is very beautiful, both from its architecture and its situation. Most of the towns in the West Riding, the largest of which is Leeds, are supported by manufactures of cloth, linen and woollen goods. Sheffield is a celebrated place for knives, scissors and cutlery of all sorts and plated goods. It is said, that it owes the excellence of its cutlery to the quality of the water, which is particularly good for tempering

YORKSHIRE.

steel. There is a great curiosity near the town of Knaresborough, called the Dripping Well. It is a little stream that runs over the surface of a rock, and drips into a kind of trough or basin beneath. The water has the power of incrusting all substances, which are soaked in it, with a stony matter. The people who live near put all kinds of things, such as birds' nests, old wigs, stuffed birds, leaves and pieces of moss, on the edge of the rock, and in a few months they seem as if they were converted into stone.

The NORTH RIDING is chiefly an agricultural district. The East part of it, called Cleveland and Holderness, is famous for its breed of horses and oxen. In this part, as well as in the West Riding, near Richmond, there is some very beautiful scenery. But the most interesting spot in the North Riding is the city of York. It was founded either by the Romans, or else before they came here. The Cathedral, or Minster, as it is generally called, is the finest building of its kind in the world, and is very ancient, having been built in the twelfth century. York Castle is still older, and was built by William the Conqueror. The Archbishop of York is called the Primate of England.

The EAST RIDING is also chiefly agricultural, but it contains the great sea-port of Hull, or Kingston-upon-Hull, as its name is written in full, which is a very important place.

Chester Cathedral

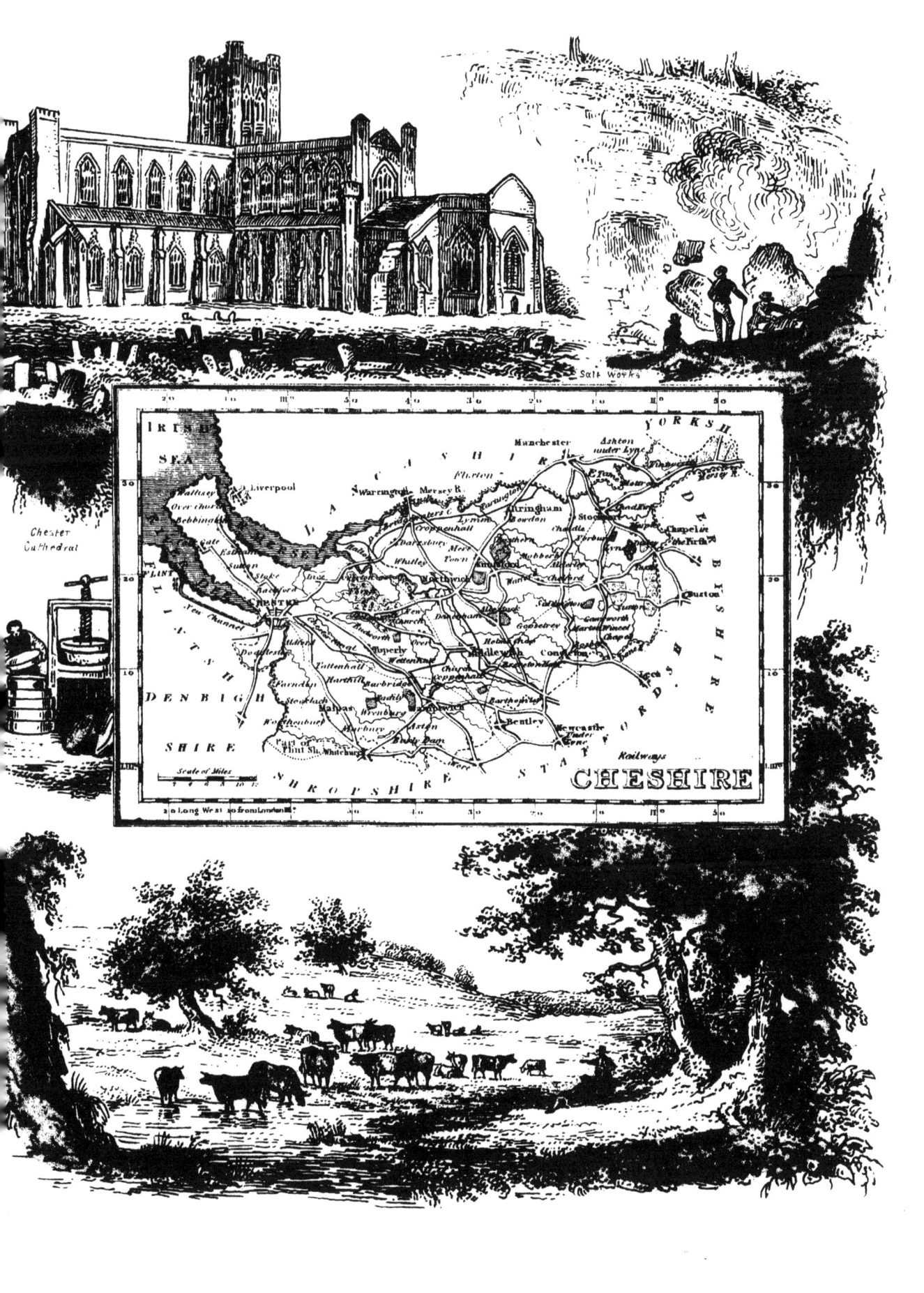

Salt Works

CHESHIRE

CHESHIRE.

This is a County Palatine, like Lancashire and Durham. The dignity of Count Palatine was held by the Earls of Chester, but it now belongs to the King of England. The length of the county is fifty-eight miles, and the width thirty-two miles. It contains 395,000 inhabitants. The city of Chester is the capital of the county.

The surface of Cheshire is generally flat, and used to be covered with extensive forests. There is now a great quantity of timber grown here, especially oak. There is not much corn produced, but the pasture is some of the finest in England. The farmers are not in the habit of growing much corn, because the grass is so much more valuable. In most of the farmers' leases, the landlords require that not more than one-fourth of the land shall be ploughed for corn. From the good quality of the grass, the Cheshire cheese has become famous. There are 100,000 cows kept in the county, which produce more than twelve thousand tons of cheese every year. The potatoes of Cheshire are very excellent, and are taken in great quantities to Liverpool.

There is plenty of coal in this county, of very good quality. But the most remarkable product is salt, which is found at Northwich, Middlewich,

CHESHIRE.

Nantwich, and other places. The greater part of it is found in the form of rock-salt, which is quarried like stone, and obtained by blasting with gunpowder. Some of it is beautifully white and clear, but generally it has a brown tinge, from its containing a small quantity of iron; and has nearly the appearance of sugar-candy. There are also brine springs, from which a large quantity of salt is manufactured by boiling and crystallizing.

The city of Chester was built by the Romans, and a great many fine remains of Roman art have been found in the neighbourhood. A few years ago there was a stone gateway, which the Romans had left; but it was pulled down because it was in the way. The general appearance of the city is very old-fashioned and remarkable. The Cathedral is not a fine structure; it was built about the time of Henry the Sixth. The Castle was built by William the First. The city walls are very fine remains of the old kind of fortification, and are rather like those of Carlisle.

The silk manufacture is carried on at Congleton; and both the silk and cotton at Stockport and Macclesfield, and other towns in the East part of the county.

There are two railways which run through the county from North to South; one called the Grand Junction, and the other the Manchester and Birmingham line.

Carlisle Cathedral

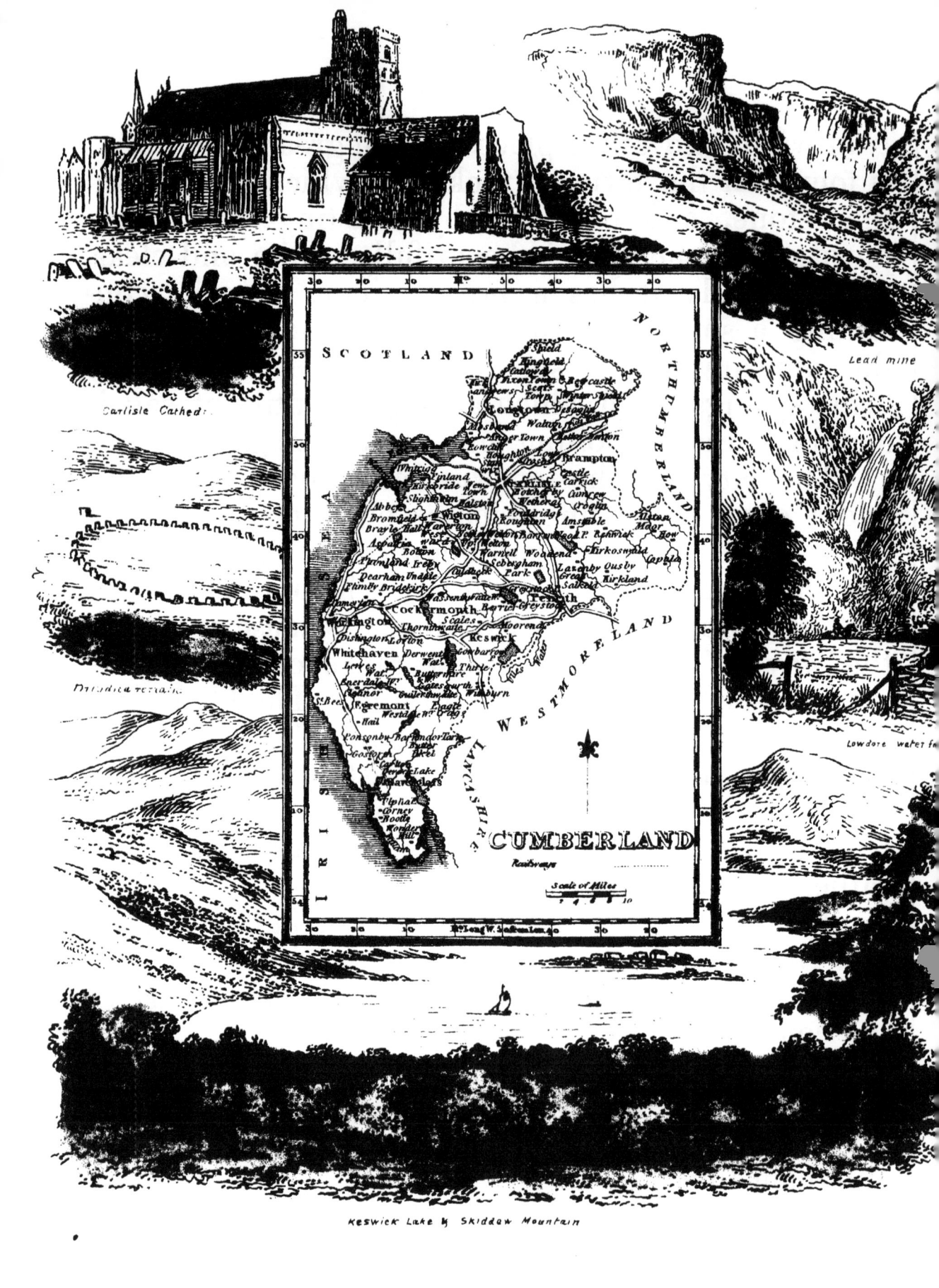

Lead mine

Druidical remains

Lowdore water fall

CUMBERLAND

Keswick Lake & Skiddaw Mountain

CUMBERLAND.

This county is seventy-four miles long and thirty-four broad. It contains 178,000 inhabitants.

Cumberland is a very mountainous part of the country; and, in consequence of this, nearly half the land in it cannot be cultivated, though sheep feed upon it. The valleys are some of them very fertile and well cultivated. The poor people are generally steady and sober; and, in consequence, they live in comfort. The chief products of the county are slate and iron, which are found in many parts; and black lead, of which there are some mines near Scafell.

The mountains and lakes make the scenery beautiful; and some of the most picturesque spots in England are in Cumberland. The most celebrated of the mountains are Skiddaw and Scafell, which is the highest mountain in England, being 3,166 feet in height. The most famous of the Cumberland lakes is Derwent Water, which is surrounded on all sides by noble mountains. There is a very curious island upon it, which floats on the surface, and has probably been formed by wood that has drifted together, and been united by grass and weeds growing upon it. On this lake may be seen the Bottom Wind, as it is called, which is a very strange thing. When there is scarcely any wind at all, and the air seems quite still, the water becomes agitated, almost as if it was boiling. This has never been clearly accounted for; but it seems likely that it arises from springs at the bottom, which, from some cause, act at times much more powerfully than is usual. Another of the attractions of Derwent Water is the waterfall of Lowdore.

When the Saxons took possession of England, Cumberland was one of the places in which the ancient Britons took shelter. Here they lived on the mountains, and in the thick forests that were then standing; and perhaps were too poor, and their land too barren, to tempt their enemies to dislodge them. One of the names by which the Britons were called was the "Cumbri," and from this word the county has its name. There are a great many British remains, but two of the most remarkable are the Druid's temples, one of which is near Keswick, and another near Penrith. The latter is called Long Meg and her daughters, and consists of a circle of sixty-six unhewn stones, and one larger one standing by itself at a little distance.

Carlisle is a city, and was built by the Britons, and destroyed by the Danes. It was afterwards restored by William Rufus, who, it is said, built the castle. During the wars between the English and Scotch, it was once taken by the Scotch, and suffered several sieges. The Cathedral is built of red sandstone, but the nave was destroyed by Oliver Cromwell, and has never been rebuilt.

DERBYSH.

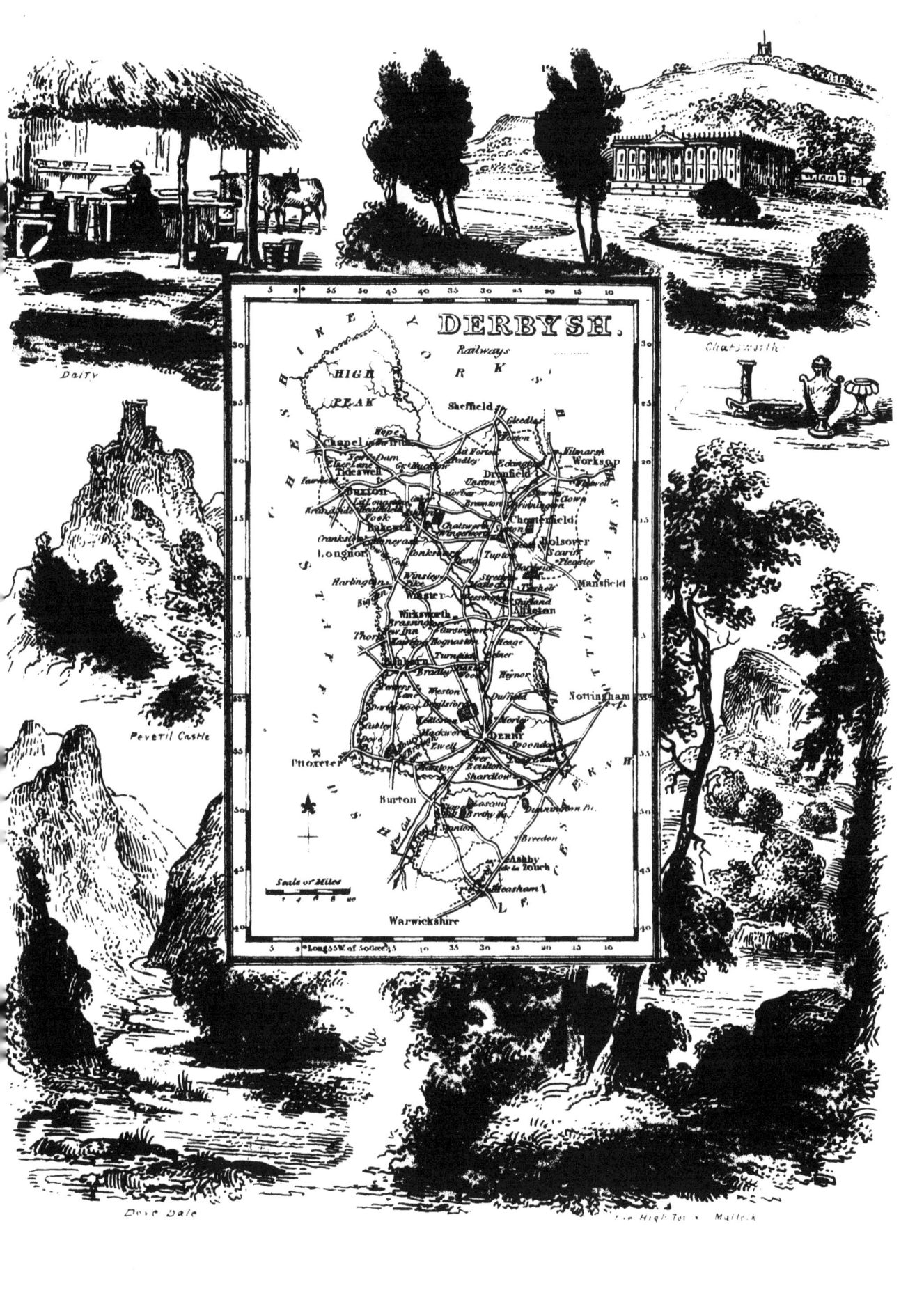

Dairy

Chatsworth

Pevetil Castle

Dove Dale

High Tor Matlock

DERBYSHIRE.

This is an inland county. It is fifty-six miles long, and thirty-four wide; and contains 272,000 people. The county town is Derby.

The South part of the county is flat and well cultivated. The produce is wheat, oats and barley, potatoes and very good cheese, though not equal to that of Cheshire.

The North portion is very different from the South. It abounds with lofty hills and abrupt rocks, streams and waterfalls; and is one of the most beautiful parts of England. There are several rivers running through it, which have their course in some parts through deep valleys, bounded by steep rocks; and it is impossible to imagine prettier scenery. The two most beautiful rivers are the Dove and the Derwent; and the most beautiful spots are Dove Dale and Matlock, near which there is a strangely shaped hill, called the High Tor. This part of the county abounds with coal, iron and lead. It is supposed that the lead mines were worked more than sixteen hundred years ago. The celebrated Derbyshire spar, or, as chemists would call it, "fluate of lime," is found in great quantities, and is worked into vases, basins, bell-pulls, candle-sticks, and many other articles.

DERBYSHIRE.

There is a high ridge, called the Peak, and on this the noted Peverel lived, in the time of William the Conqueror. The ruins of his castle are still there, and are called the Peak Castle. Not many miles from this, is Chatsworth, the magnificent estate and house of the Duke of Devonshire. The river Derwent flows through the park, which is ten miles in circumference, and is one of the most beautiful parks in England. Mary, Queen of Scots, spent the greater part of her long captivity on this spot. The present mansion was finished in the year 1706.

There are some Druidical remains in Derbyshire, and several curiously shaped natural stones, which have been taken for Druid's altars, without being so. The Romans had several stations in this county, which they seem to have considered an important spot, perhaps, from the lead and iron that it produced. They founded the town of Derby, and many Roman remains have been discovered in and near it. It is now a famous place for the manufacture of silk, and was the first place in England in which that art was carried on. It had before been exercised in no part of Europe except Italy, and had been kept a profound secret. But a man, named Lombe, succeeded in getting the secret from the Italian spinners, and opened a silk mill at Derby in the reign of George the Second.

LANCASHIRE.

This county is about eighty miles in length, and forty in breadth. It is the most populous county of England, and contains 1,667,000 persons. Lancaster is the county town.

Like Durham and Cheshire, this is a County Palatine; that is, the Duke of Lancaster, or Lord of the County, has authority in the county, like that of the King, in regard to the punishment of offenders and other particulars. But since the reign of Henry IV., who was previously Duke of Lancaster, this authority has belonged to the King, though it belongs to him by a distinct right as Duke of Lancaster, and not as King of England.

The North part of the county, which is separated from the rest, is called Furness. It contains some mountains and lakes, and there are also in it the interesting ruins of Furness Abbey. A large portion of the rest of the county is flat, and in some parts it is marshy.

Lancaster was a Roman town, and gave its name to the county, and derives its own name from the river Lume on which it stands, and the latin "Castra," a camp. The castle is a fine old structure, and part of it was built in the time of King Edward the Third.

LANCASHIRE.

Liverpool and Manchester are the two largest towns in England next to London. Liverpool contains 223,000 inhabitants, and Manchester 192,000.

Liverpool is a great place for shipping, and has some of the most extensive docks in the world. It is situated on the river Mersey, and does not appear to have existed as a town till after the time of William the Conqueror. In the year 1700, its population was only 35,600. You may judge from this how rapidly it has increased. The number of ships which are unloaded every year at Liverpool, amounts to 15,000. One great branch of the trade is cotton, which is brought from America and the West Indies, and sent by the railway to Manchester, where it is manufactured into calico and other articles. The most considerable of the inhabitants of Liverpool are merchants.

Manchester is full of factories, and its most considerable inhabitants are manufacturers. It is a very ancient place, having been founded by the Romans. There is a very fine church here, which is shortly to become a Cathedral, and Manchester will then be a city.

There are many other large town in Lancashire, which are supported by manufactures, particularly of cotton goods, which are made better here than in any other part of the world.

LANCASHIRE

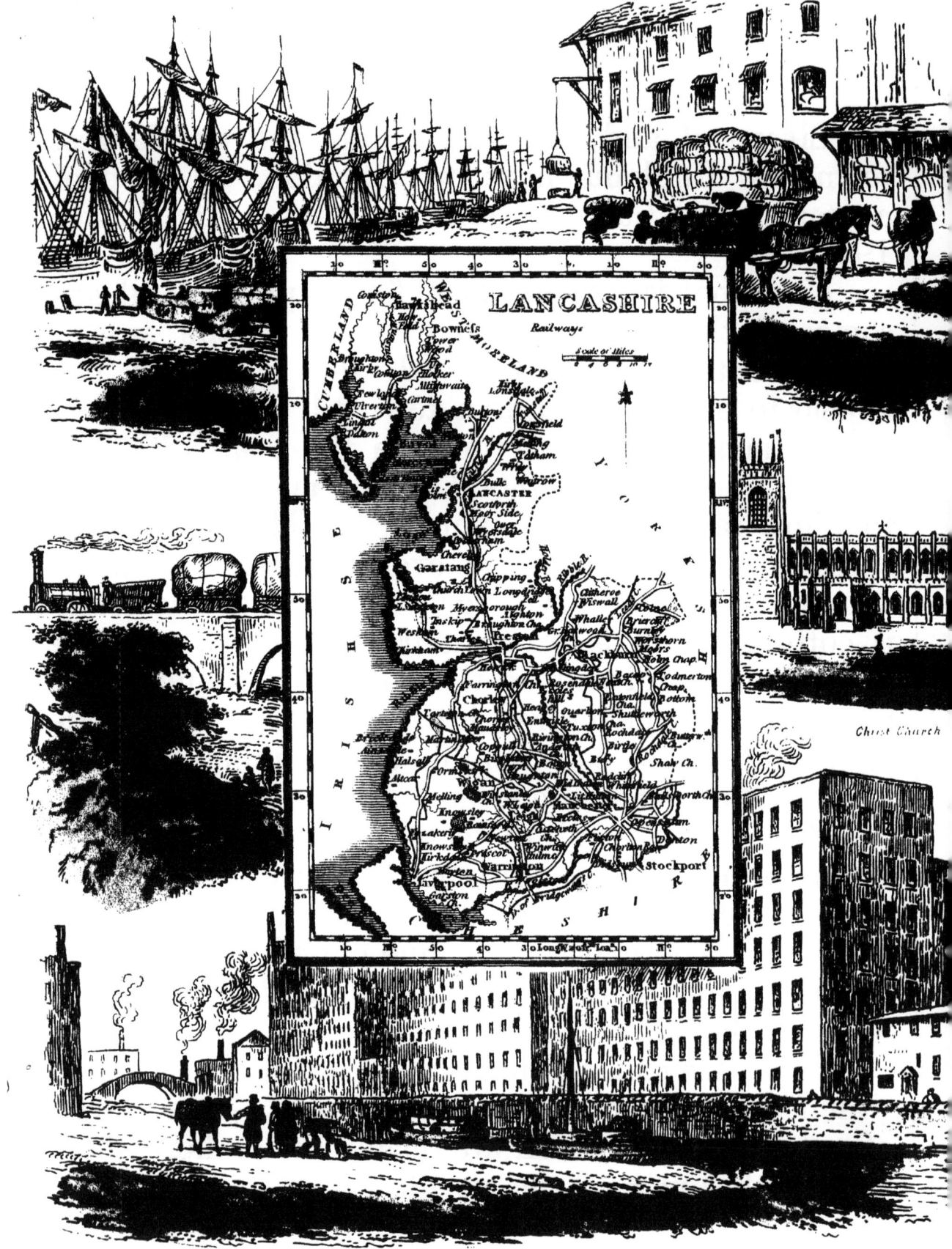

Christ Church

Cotton Mills

NORTHUMBERLAND.

This is the most Northern part of England, except the small part of Durham, which is separated from the rest of the county, and forms the North corner of England. Northumberland is seventy miles in length, and forty-seven miles in width. The population is 250,000. The county town is Newcastle.

The climate of Northumberland is cold; and, in consequence, the crops are late. But the farmers cultivate their land very well, and obtain a large quantity of wheat and other produce. The horses, oxen and sheep, which are bred here, are of a very hardy kind, such as can bear hard work and cold weather.

The most important production of the county is coal, which is better in this county and Durham than in any other part of England. This kind of coal is often called in the South of England Sea coal, or Sea-borne coal, because it comes to London and other places by sea. There is a different kind produced in the midland counties, which, instead of burning into a hard bright cinder, turns to dry ashes. The coals are taken from the mines, and generally brought by small railways to the river Tyne, where they are put on board ship. From the two counties of Northumberland and Durham there

NORTHUMBERLAND.

are taken every year six millions and a half of tons of coals to different parts of England.

Northumberland was anciently united with the other counties North of the river Humber, in the kingdom of Northumberland, which was one of the states of the Saxon Heptarchy. The name, as you may see, means, "the land North of the Humber." In the time of Edward the Confessor, the same district formed the earldom of the great Earl Siward, who fought against the Scotch usurper Macbeth, of which you may read in Shakspere.

Amongst the curiosities of this county, are the remains of the Roman wall, built to defend the county against the Picts, who inhabited Scotland.

The parts of Newcastle that have lately been built, are some of the finest streets in England. But one of the most interesting places in the county is Hexham. It was founded when the Romans were in England, and was once a city. There was a large priory here, a very fine building, of which a great part of the church is still standing. There was also a large priory at Tynemouth, of which the ruins may be seen boldly standing out upon a rock, overhanging the sea. There are in the county a great many fine old castles, of which I can only give you the names of a few. Alnwick Castle, where the Duke of Northumberland now lives; Warkworth Castle; Bothwell Castle; Langley Castle, and a number of others.

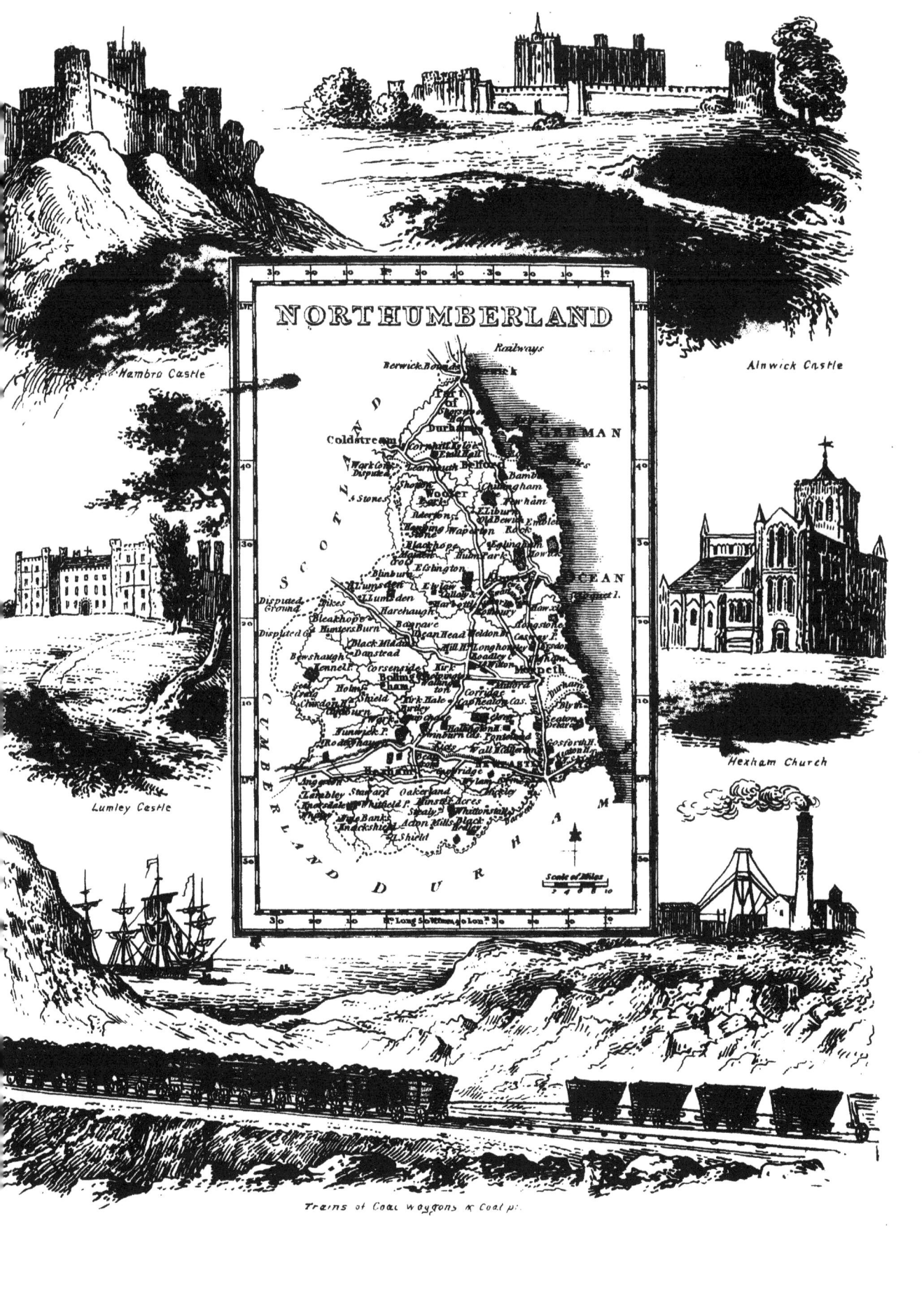

NORTHUMBERLAND

Hambro Castle

Alnwick Castle

Lumley Castle

Hexham Church

Trains of Coal waggons & Coal p[its]

DURHAM.

The part of the county of Durham contained in the map is forty-eight miles long and thirty-nine miles wide. There are two other small portions, one near Morpeth, in Northumberland; and the other bordering on Scotland, being the North point of England, and including Holy Island. The population of the whole of Durham is 324,000. The city of Durham is the capital of the county, but Sunderland is a much larger place.

The soil of Durham is not fertile, though the cows that are bred here are famed all over England. But the most valuable productions of the county are coal and lead. You will find something respecting the coal of this part in the account of Northumberland. The most important ports for shipping it are Shields, Sunderland and Stockton. The lead ore contains a small proportion of silver, which is carefully separated from it.

Durham was originally, like Cheshire and Lancashire, a County Palatine; that is, the Lord of the county had authority in the county almost equal to that of the King. From the time of the conquest, this dignity was held by the Bishops of Durham; but in the reign of William the Fourth, it was taken away, and is now held by the king.

DURHAM.

The city of Durham is very beautifully situated on a small hill, which it covers, and which is nearly surrounded by the river Wear. The Cathedral stands on the highest part of the hill, and forms a noble object as you approach the city. It is a fine building, and is very ancient, having been built during the reigns of William Rufus and Henry the First. The original see of the Bishop of this diocese was Holy Island, or Lindisfarne, where there are now some interesting ruins; but, as the Danes often invaded the coast, this was considered insecure, and the Bishop and Clergy removed to Chester-le-Street, and there began to build a Cathedral. But as the Danes attacked this part too, the Bishop went to Ripon, in Yorkshire, which has lately become a Bishop's see again; and lastly they came to Durham, where the Bishopric has continued ever since.

There is a University at Durham, which was founded by the Dean and Canons of the Cathedral in the year 1831.

Berwick-upon-Tweed, which is situated to the North of the North part of Durham, is a very curious place, for it is in no county, neither is it in England or Scotland. It was once a very rich place and strongly fortified. It has always had a kind of independence; and when Edward the First granted it a charter, similar to those of other English borough towns, he allowed it to retain the old Scotch laws.

Durham Cathedral

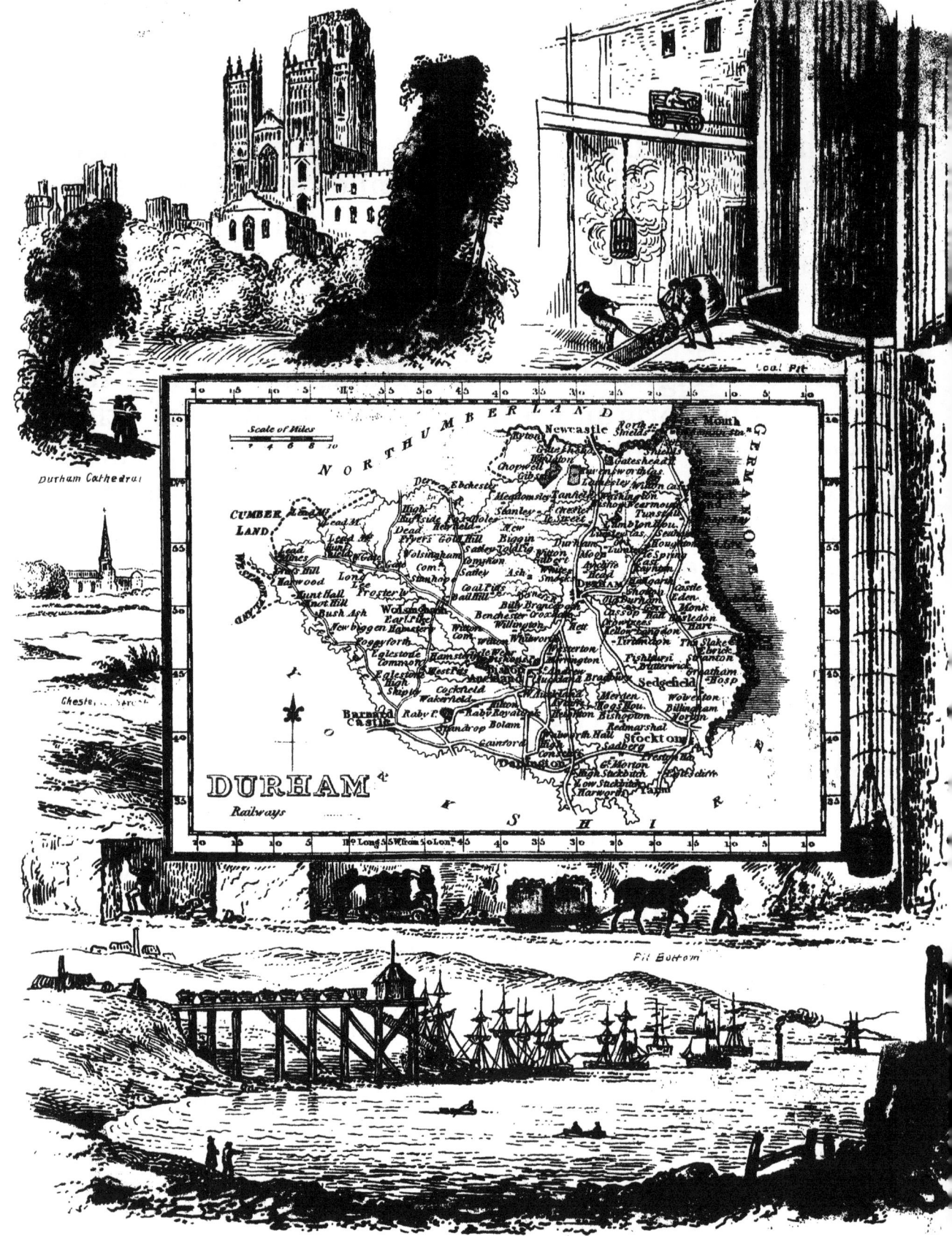

Coal Pit

DURHAM
Railways

Pit Bottom

Shipping Coal

WESTMORELAND.

This county is forty miles from East to West, and thirty-three miles from North to South. It contains 56,000 persons. The county town is Appleby. The county has its name from its being on the "West" side of England, consisting chiefly of "moor" land, which is very barren. It produces slate and a bad sort of coal.

The scenery in this county is very beautiful, and the lakes are the finest in England. Of these, the largest is Windermere, or Winandermere, which is eleven miles long, and about two miles wide. In some places it is more than one hundred and eighty feet deep. But the scenery of Ulleswater is still more beautiful. Grasmere and Rydalmere are also very beautiful, but much smaller. In most of the lakes there are small islands, covered with trees; and the water abounds with fine fish. All round the lakes are lofty mountains, the tallest of which is Helvellyn, that stands partly in Cumberland. It is more than 3000 feet in height. It was on this mountain that a young man perished some years ago. He started to go over the mountain without a guide, accompanied by a little dog. A snow storm came on, and as he did not know his way, he most likely wandered about till he sunk down, quite tired out, and died. Many days afterwards his body was found, and by it stood his faithful dog, who had lived, no one knows how, while he was watching the remains of his master. The Poet Wordsworth, has written a beautiful poem on this incident, called Fidelity; and Sir Walter Scott wrote another, entitled Helvellyn. Both these poems are well worth your reading.

There are a great many waterfalls in Westmoreland; but the one which pleased me most is that called Dungeon Gyll, which is in a deep cleft of one of the two mountains, called the Langdale Pikes. You look into a narrow space, between two high and straight walls of rock; and, in the inner end, the stream falls down from a great height, into a deep basin beneath, where the water looks beautifully pure and clear.

Some of the most beautiful objects in the county are the Tarns, or little lakes, upon the mountains. These are generally quite small, very deep, and the water is as clear as crystal; but, owing to the depth, looking in the middle quite black.

You ought to know, that the names of the mountains and lakes of Westmoreland and Cumberland are old British names; for this was one of the counties into which the Britons were driven by the Saxons, and where they lived for a long time. The word "Mere" signifies a lake; "Gyll," or "Force," means a waterfall; and "Tarn," a small lake.

Brough Castle

Stock-gill Force

Slate Quarry

WESTMORELAND

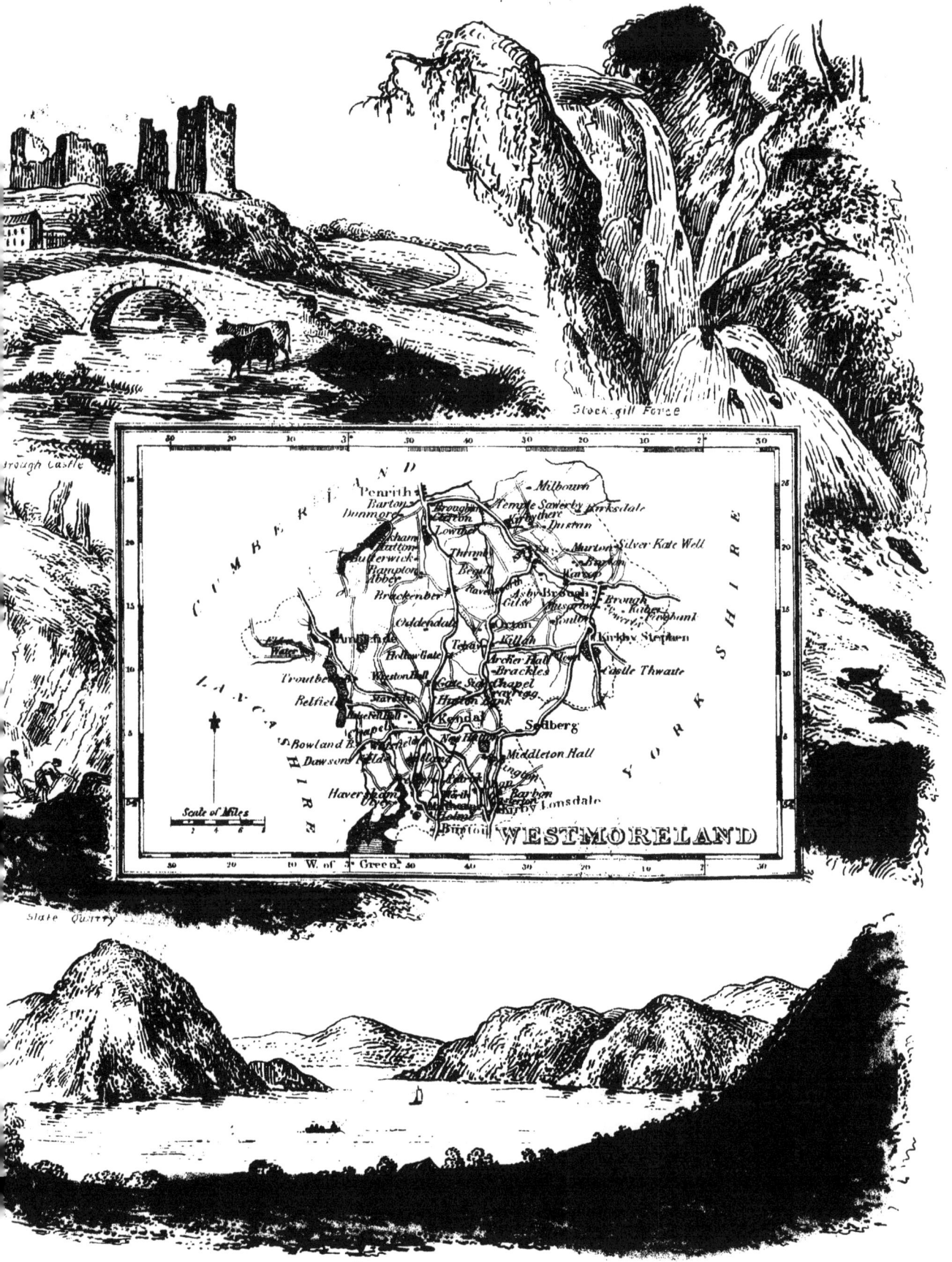

Ullswater Lake

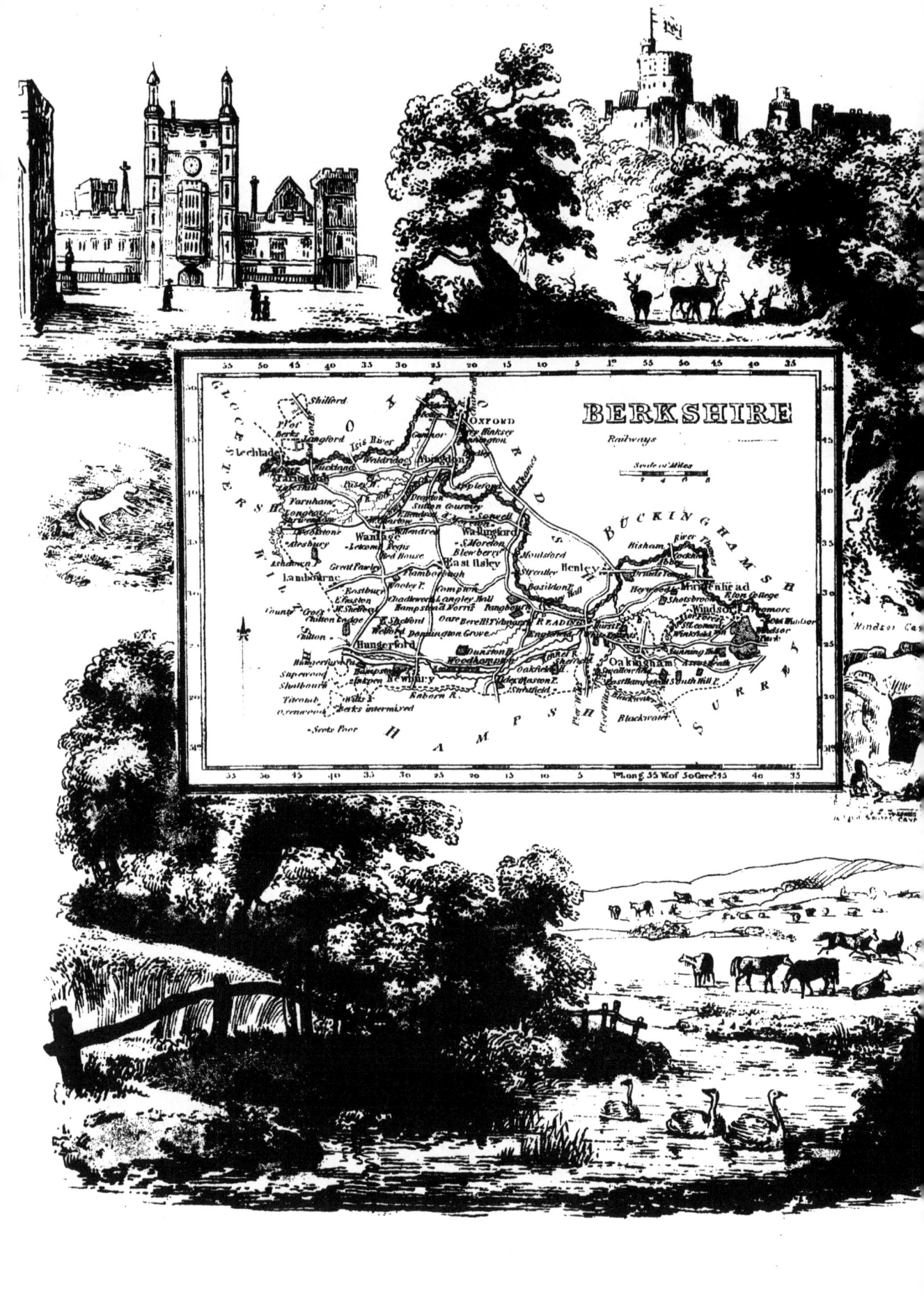

BERKSHIRE

BERKSHIRE.

The scenery of some parts of the county of Berkshire, or Barkshire as it used to be called, is very beautiful, and abounds with fine woods and pastures. The river Thames runs quite through the county from East to West, and so does the Great Western Railway. It contains 160,000 inhabitants.

Windsor Castle is the finest royal palace in England, and the Queen stays there the greater part of the time that she does not spend in London. It is a magnificent place—one of the most interesting in the world. It was built by King Edward the Third. The park is very large and very beautiful, abounding with large trees, and containing plenty of fine deer. There is a part of the castle called the round tower, from the top of which there is a noble view of the surrounding country.

In the castle there is a very fine collection of paintings. There is also a very curious armoury, containing the weapons and armour of a great many kings and great men, who have fought in the cause

BERKSHIRE.

of their country. Every one of our kings, since Edward the Third, has spent a good deal of time in this palace; and it is a place which all Englishmen should visit who have it in their power.

Near the town of Newbury, there are the ruins of Donnington Castle, which are pleasantly situated on a woody hill. The castle was built in the time of Richard the Second, and was so knocked about in the civil wars, that only the gateway and two towers are now standing. But what makes this spot most interesting is, that Geoffry Chaucer, the great poet, lived here for some time.

There are many remains of ancient British and Roman work in this county. One very remarkable object is called Wayland Smith's cave, which is not far from Lambourn. It was most likely a Druid's temple; but the country people say that it was built by an invisible blacksmith, named Wayland Smith, who now works in it by night.

There is not far from this spot, the figure of a white horse rudely cut out on the side of a chalk hill. It is supposed that this was formed to commemorate a victory gained over the Danes by Ethelred and Alfred.

DORSETSH.

DORSETSHIRE.

The county of Dorset contains about 174,000 inhabitants. It abounds with rich pasture land, and produces a great quantity of butter. Flax and hemp are cultivated in several parts of the county.

Stone is a very important product of Dorsetshire, and it is quarried in many parts of the coast: the best kind is called Portland stone, and comes from the island of Portland. This sort is chiefly used for building. A coarser kind comes from Purbeck, and is employed chiefly for paving the streets. There is also a kind of marble found at Purbeck, of of which the pillars in many of our old cathedrals are formed. Some fine specimens of it are to be seen in the Temple Church in London.

The cliffs of the more Western part of the coast of this county, produce the stones from which Roman cement is made. These cliffs, in the neighbourhood of the town of Lyme Regis, are nearly full of curious fossils; the most remarkable of which are the bones of the large reptiles called Icthyosaurus and

DORSETSHIRE.

Plesiosaurus, and skeletons of these are represented at the top of the plate. The Icthyosaurus was something like a crocodile; but, instead of having feet, it had fins like those of a whale: it appears therefore that it could not walk on land. It had large eyes with very strong powers of sight; as is known from their resemblance to the eye of the eagle. The name Icthyosaurus is formed of two Greek words signifying "fish-lizard." It was sometimes more than thirty feet long.

The Plesiosaurus also had fins, but it was not so large or so strong as the Icthyosaurus. It had a very long neck, much longer even than that of the swan. The head was small and very weak, compared with the other. Its length varied from six to fifteen feet. The name signifies "like a lizard."

The remains of these wonderful creatures are collected from the cliffs by Miss Anning, whose collection all should go to see who go to Lyme Regis.

Corfe Castle is a very extensive ruin of a strong castle, built on the top of a hill by King Edgar: it is not far from Poole, a town which once carried on a large trade in salt fish, brought from Newfoundland, but which has now very much declined.

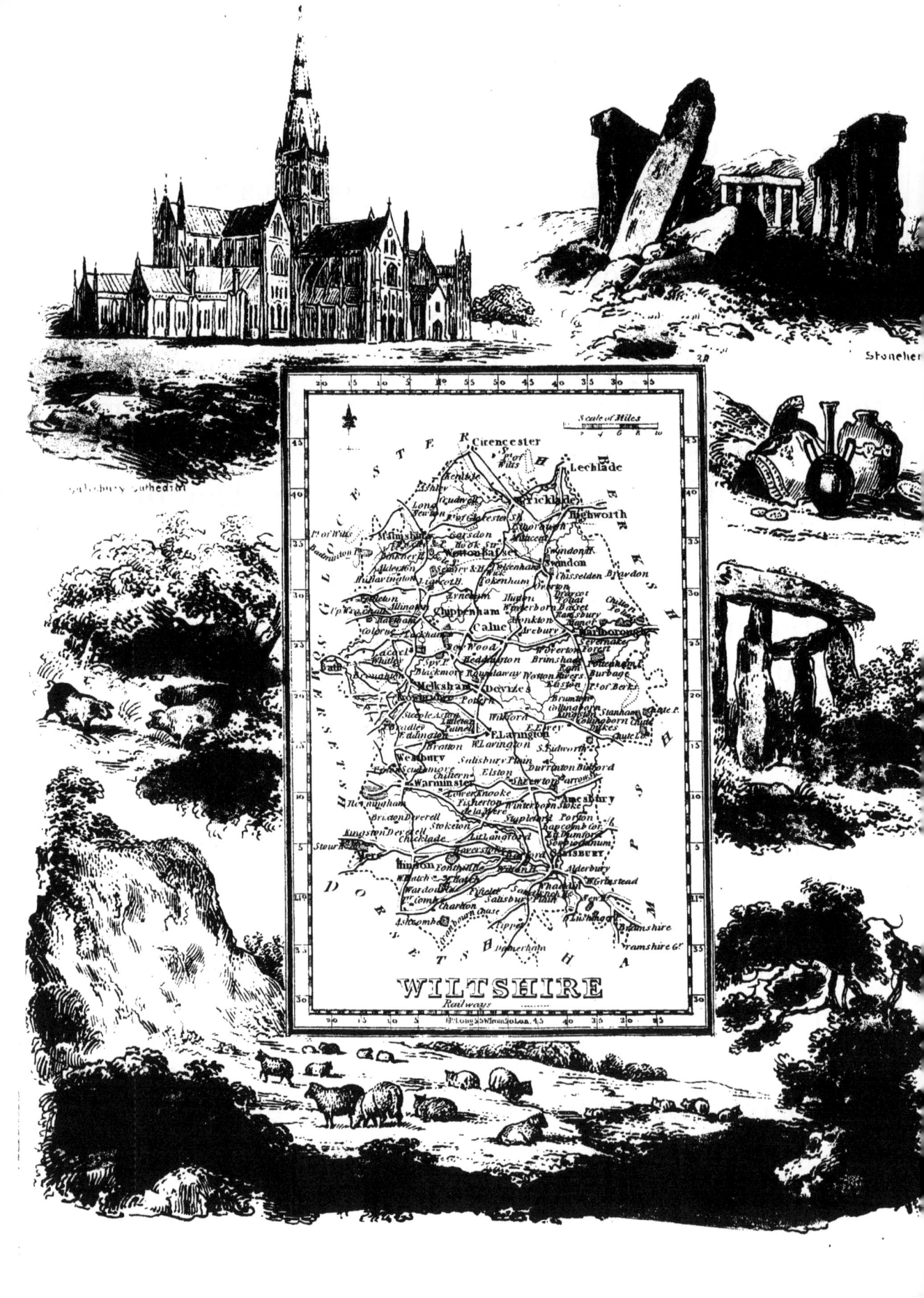

WILTSHIRE

WILTSHIRE.

Wiltshire is an inland county, which contains 260,000 people. There is a great deal of chalk in it, and the surface of a large part of this is very bare of trees, and produces little besides short grass. This part of the county is called Salisbury Plain, and a great many sheep are fed upon it. The Northern portion is more thickly wooded, and in some parts very fine pigs are produced.

Some years ago there was a considerable quantity of carpet and cloth made in this county, particularly in the town of Wilton. But these manufactures have of late fallen off, and most of the carpet and cloth we use, is now made in the North of England.

The capital of Wiltshire is the city of Salisbury, which contains about 13,000 inhabitants. The Cathedral is a very beautiful building, and the spire is the highest in England. It was built in the reign of King Henry the Third.

Nearly close to Salisbury there is a very curious place, called Old Sarum. It is a low mound of earth, surrounded by a bank. It was once a Roman fortress, and in it the old Cathedral stood. But in

WILTSHIRE.

consequence of the captain and soldiers who kept it annoying the Bishop and Clergy, it was determined to erect the new one in its present situation.

The city of Salisbury is famous for the manufacture of knives, scissars, and other cutlery. It is said that the water of the place is particularly good for the tempering of steel.

The most wonderful things in the county are the two great druidical temples of Abury, or Avebury, and Stonehenge. The temple of Abury is the more extensive of the two, but the stones are much smaller, and there is not nearly so much of it remaining. Stonehenge is the most interesting monument of the kind in the world. It consists of very large stones, which were formerly placed in two circles, one within the other, cross stones being laid upon the tops of others placed upright, so as to unite them. The greater number of the stones are of a white sandstone, such as is found on the Marlborough Downs, about twelve miles off; but a few are of granite and black marble. They are rudely squared, and are fitted together by what carpenters call a mortice and tenon. Stonehenge stands near the middle of Salisbury Plain.

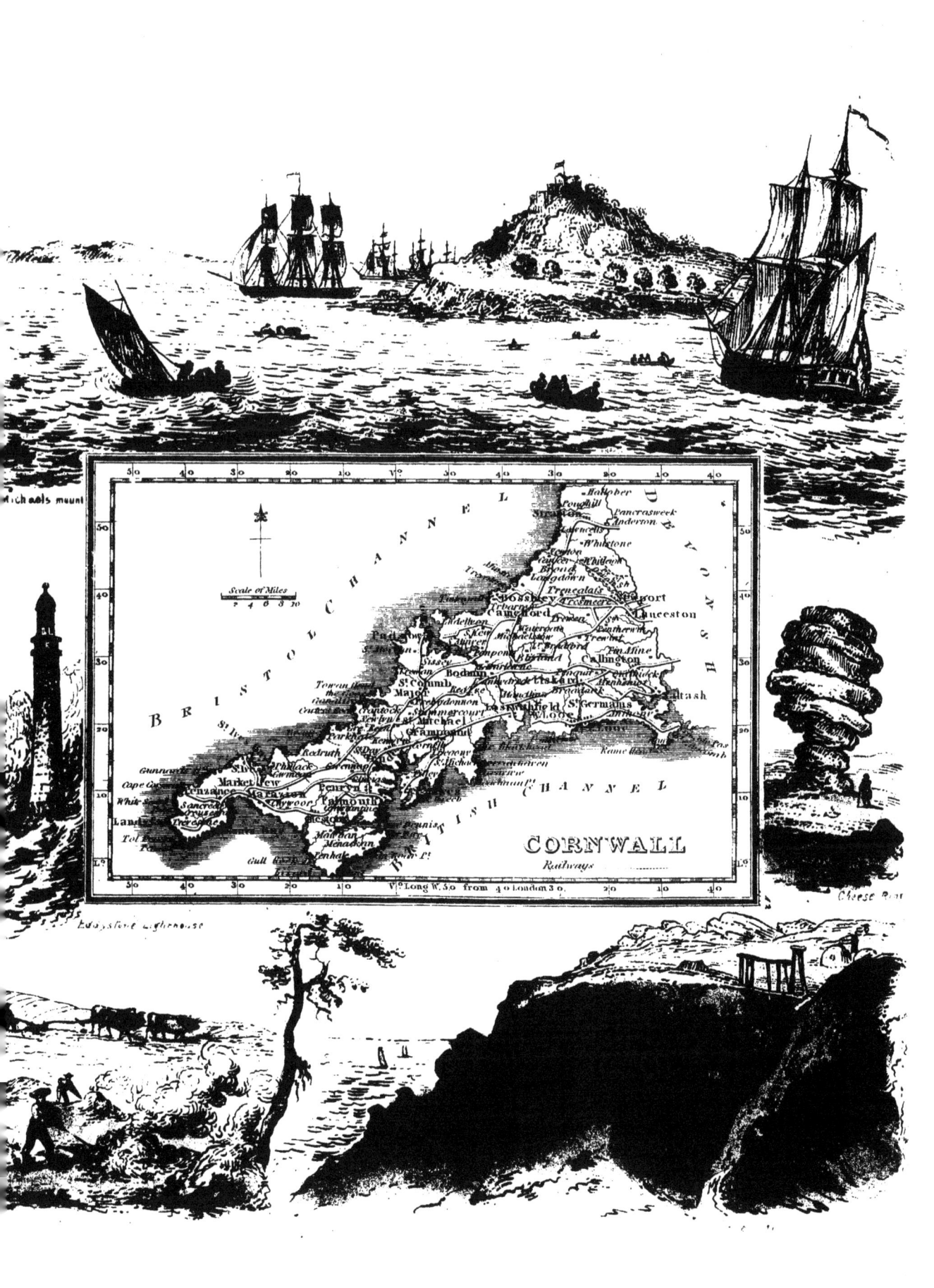

CORNWALL

CORNWALL.

This county is at the South-Western extremity of England, and it is surrounded by the sea on three sides. The population is 341,000. The dukedom of Cornwall has always belonged to the eldest son of the king, since the time of Edward the Black Prince, and he has peculiar authority in the county. There is an officer under him called the Lord Warden of the Stannary Courts; and in these courts all causes connected with the mines are tried. The word Stannary comes from the Latin "stannum," tin.

The greater part of the land of Cornwall is barren; but in some spots it is famous for the growth of potatoes. A few places are rendered fertile by collecting sea-weed, mixing it with turf and weeds, and then burning it: this produces an excellent manure. There is but little wood; and in several parts, of considerable extent, there is scarcely anything to be seen on the surface but bare rocks of granite and slate.

There is no part of England which is so famous for producing metals as Cornwall. It abounds with copper, lead and tin, and produces also silver and antimony. One of the most remarkable of the mines is the Botallick Copper Mine, the entrance to which is represented in the plate. It extends a long distance quite under the bed of the sea.

St. Michael's Mount is a hill which rises from the sand of the shore, and at high tide it is surrounded by water. It is said to have been the place to which the Phenicians used to come, 2000 years ago, to purchase tin of the Britons, but this is not certainly known. For several centuries it was inhabited by monks; and the place was regarded with such reverence, that people who wished to show their repentance for their sins, used to come to it as pilgrims. Afterwards it was strongly fortified, and was taken and retaken in the civil wars. There are now about 200 people living on it.

Some of the rocks of Cornwall are of such strange shapes, that it has been doubted whether they owe their form to nature or art. The most remarkable of these is the Cheese-Ring; and another is the Logan or rocking stone, which, although it weighs several tons, may be moved by a touch.

The famous Eddystone Lighthouse stands on some sunken rocks off the coast of Cornwall.

HAMPSHIRE.

Hampshire contains 354,000 inhabitants: its capital is the city of Winchester. The county includes the Isle of Wight.

The scenery of Hampshire is very pretty and interesting: the North part abounds with long chalk ridges and beech woods; while a great part of the Southern half of the county is occupied by the New Forest, which is one of the noblest forests in England. It was either originally planted or very much enlarged by William the Conqueror, who (it is said) tyrannically turned out a great many people from their homes and destroyed many churches, in order that he might have his way, and get a good place to hunt in. His son, William Rufus, was killed while hunting in this forest. An arrow, shot by a gentleman named Walter Tyrrell, glanced against a tree, and shot the king in his breast.

The New Forest is famous for fine pigs, and a very useful hardy sort of ponies, which are bred there: it also abounds with deer. The scenery in it is some of the finest of its kind in the country.

HAMPSHIRE.

Winchester is a very fine old city, and few places contain a greater number of interesting buildings. The Cathedral is large, and built in a grand style, and is of very great antiquity. The College is also a fine old building. There is a very beautiful Cross, and several fine Churches; and at the distance of about a mile and a-half, stands the Hospital of St. Cross, which is a delightful place, built for the accommodation of a certain number of old men, who have a weekly allowance of money. The custom is kept up here of giving, to all who ask for it, a slice of bread and half-a-pint of good beer. What I have mentioned are not half the curiosities of Winchester, which was a very famous place in the time of the Saxons, and existed long before they came to England.

Southampton is a very handsome town, with a fine port and very ancient walls. In the principal street there is a fine gate of great antiquity called Bargate, and over it are the pictures of two giants. Near Southampton are the beautiful ruins of Netley Abbey.

Portsmouth, Portsea and Gosport are three towns close together, with a fine harbour, and extensive dock-yards for the building of ships of war. Portsmouth is very strongly fortified.

HAMPSHIRE

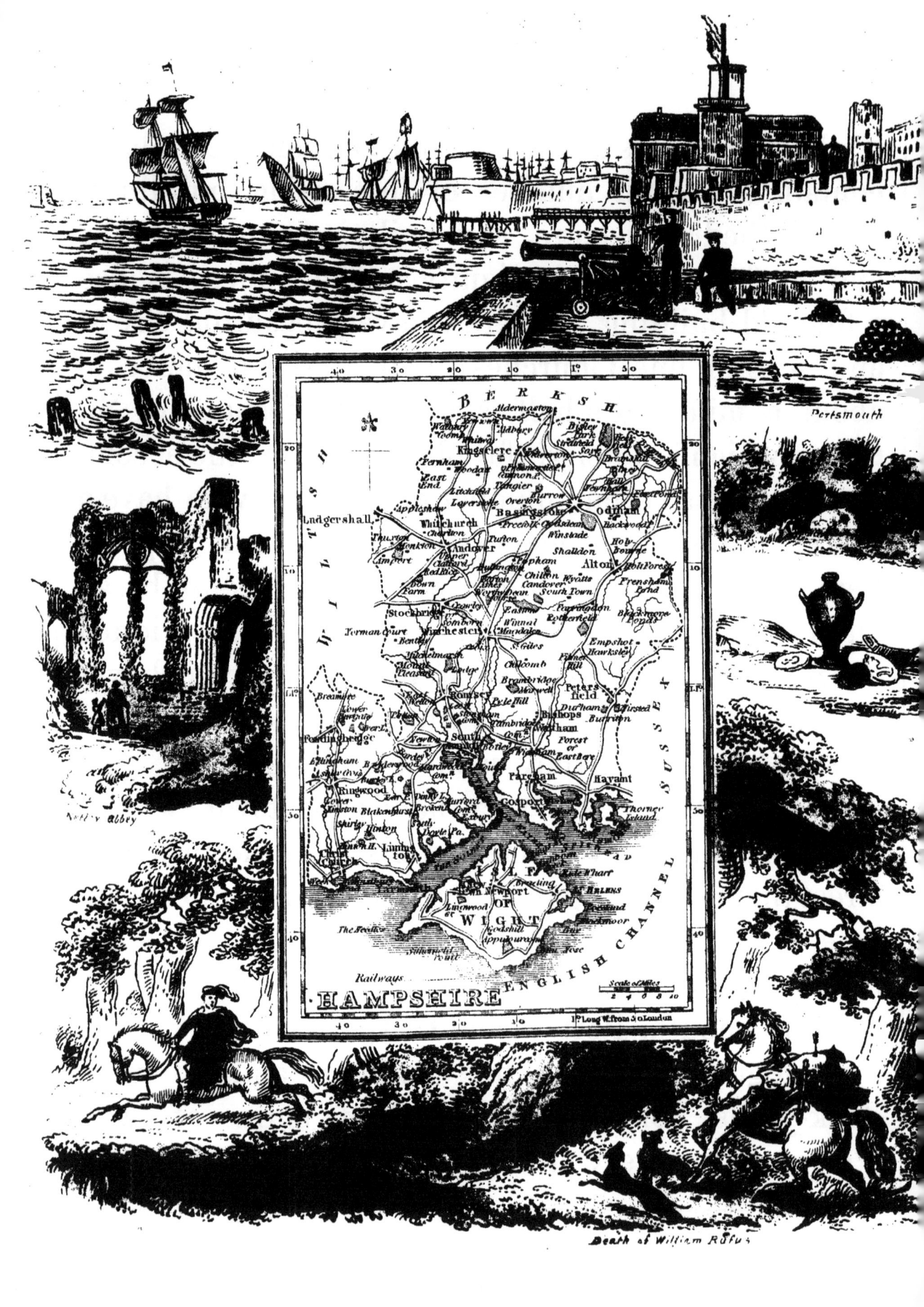

Portsmouth

Netley Abbey

Death of William Rufus

GLOUCESTERSHIRE.

Gloucestershire contains 431,000 inhabitants. It contains the city of Gloucester, and part of the city of Bristol: the two cities are united in one See, and the Bishop is called the Bishop of Gloucester and Bristol.

Gloucestershire comprises some of the most fertile spots in England. Its produce is very various. The land affords wood, fruit and corn in abundance; and the rivers plenty of fish. But the most famous of all its productions is cheese, which is so good that it is inferior to none made in England, except the Stilton and Cheshire.

Coal is found in some parts of the county, and iron mines used to be worked here; but as the metal became scarce, they fell into disuse.

Gloucester is well situated, and carries on considerable trade. It was once celebrated for the manufacture of pins. It is very ancient, and remains of Roman art are to be found in and near it. Several of the public buildings are handsome. The Cathedral, which is dedicated to St. Peter, is not only handsome, but interesting as containing specimens of many different styles. It appears to have been built at various periods during nearly four centuries, from 1050 to 1450. It contains some interesting monuments, and amongst others, those of Robert Duke of Normandy, son of William the Conqueror, and of the unhappy King Edward the Second.

Cheltenham is a town of remarkable beauty, which has rapidly increased during the last few years, owing to some medical springs which rise here. The waters are particularly good for liver complaints, and for those people who have suffered from the effects of hot climates. The town is handsomely built, with rows of trees on each side of the principal streets. This gives it a very pretty and singular appearance. Its situation is also favourable, for it stands in the midst of a fertile plain surrounded by tall hills, and from the tops of these hills there are fine views of the neighbouring country.

The scenery of the side of Gloucestershire next to Wales, includes the Malvern hills, and is extremely beautiful, and in some parts grand.

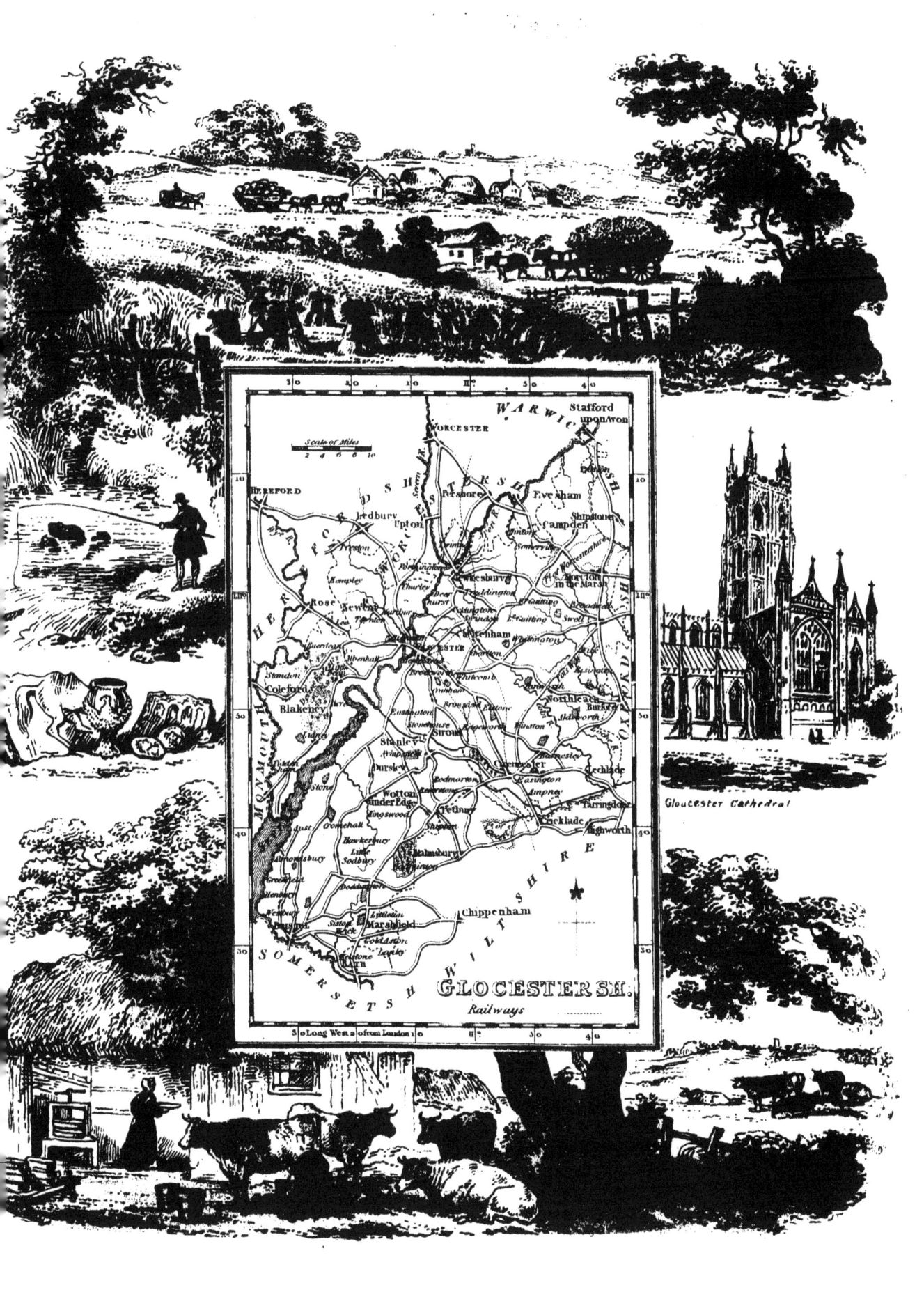

Gloucester Cathedral

GLOCESTERSH.
Railways

DEVONSHIRE.

This is the third in size of the English counties, Yorkshire being the largest and Lincolnshire the second. Its length is seventy miles, and its width about the same. It contains 534,000 inhabitants. The capital is the city of Exeter.

The scenery of Devonshire is very beautiful, and not less so on the North coast than on the South coast, or inland than by the sea side. Beautiful hills and woods and rivers are to be seen in many parts, with rich pasture and smiling orchards. Much of the land that is cultivated is on the tops and sides of very steep hills, and the produce can only be brought down on the backs of horses. This appears very strange to one who has been used only to level country. The pasture is generally very good; and the red cows of Devonshire are famous for the milk they give, but which is more remarkable for its rich quality than its quantity. Clouted cream, which is a kind of butter made by boiling the cream, is almost peculiar to Devonshire. There are some very excellent sheep fed on the hills.

There are a great number of apples and other

fruits grown in this county; and it has been remarked that the fruit trees grow here much more vigorously than in other parts of England, so that they look almost like forest trees. Most Devonshire people drink cider, as they get it better than in any other county, from the fine quality of the fruit.

Exeter is a city and county of itself, so that it has several privileges apart from the rest of the county like Southampton and some other places. The Castle, which was built, or very much improved, by William the Conqueror, is now in ruins. The Cathedral is very ancient, but it has been considerably altered from time to time. The Western front is considered to be one of the richest pieces of architecture of its kind existing, and some other parts of the building are very fine.

Plymouth, Devonport and Stonehome are a group of towns close together, in some degree resembling Portsmouth, Portsea and Gosport. Like them, they have a fine harbour, docks, and a dockyard where ships are built for the navy. In order to improve the harbour, a vast work has been built called Plymouth Break-Water, which is one of the most remarkable things of its kind in the world.

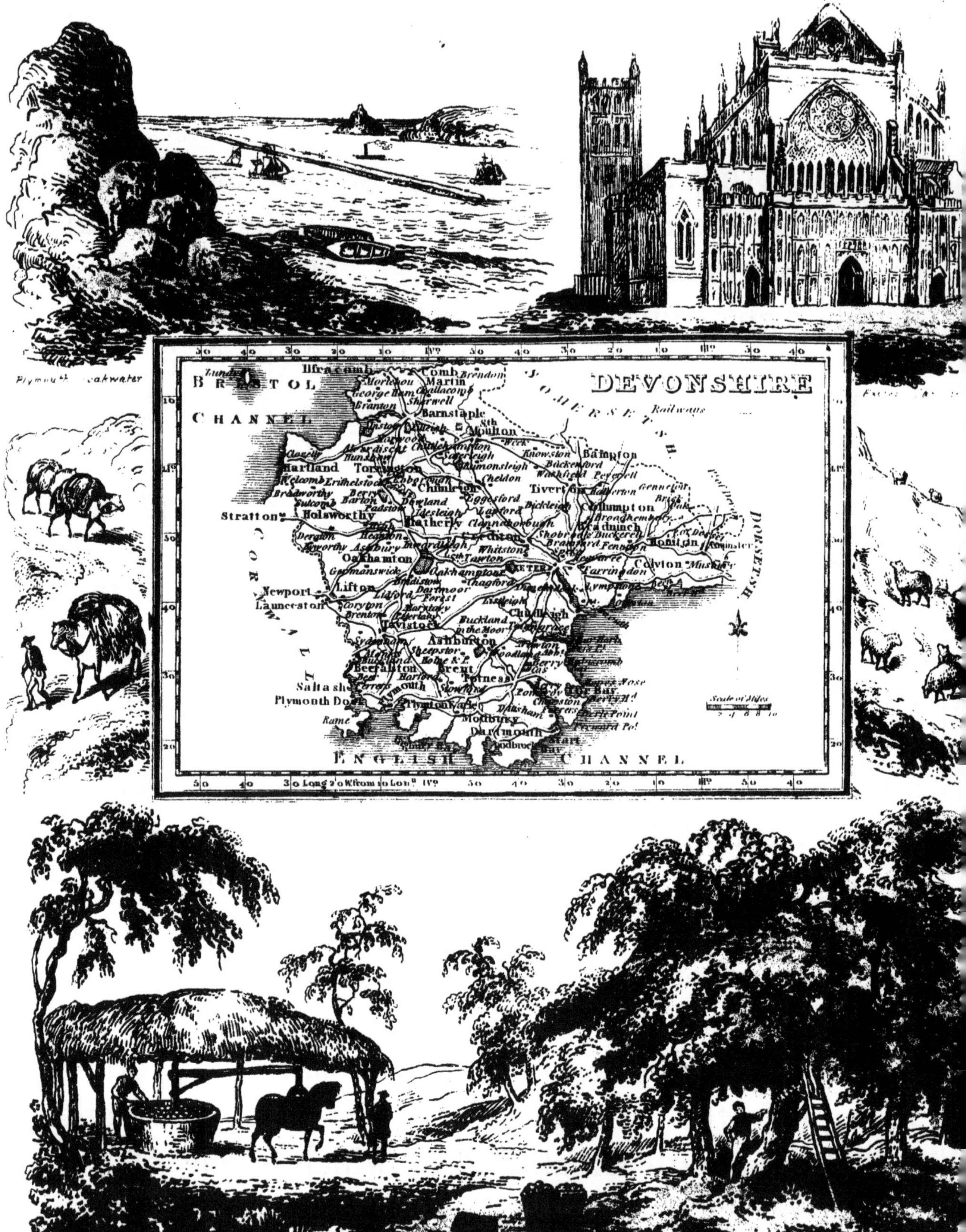
DEVONSHIRE
BRISTOL CHANNEL
ENGLISH CHANNEL
Railways
Scale of Miles
Ilfracomb
Barnstaple
Bampton
Torrington
Hartland
Holsworthy
Stratton
Tiverton
Cullumpton
Crediton
Oakhampton
Honiton
Colyton
Newport
Launceston
Lifton
Tavistock
Ashburton
Beeralston
Saltash
Plymouth Dock
Chudleigh
Totness
Modbury
Dartmouth
Dartmoor Forest
Long. 2° W. from Lon.

SOMERSETSHIRE.

This is a large county, and contains 436,000 people: it contains the cities of Bath and Wells, and part of Bristol.

The soil of Somersetshire is for the most part very fertile, and its produce is various. A great quantity of cheese is made in it. The scenery of the North part, and especially near Bristol, is remarkably fine, comprising tall hills, and rocks, and cliffs, with a fine river running at their feet. There are few spots to be preferred to Clifton for beauty.

The city of Bristol has a large shipping trade. Many parts of the county produce coal in abundance. At one time, there were very considerable manufactures of several kinds carried on here; but of late they have fallen off, and gloves now form one of the principal articles of manufacture. Yeovil is the most famous place for them.

The Cathedral of Wells is a very handsome one, and is considered a fine specimen of architecture. Bath is the chief city of Somersetshire. It is a very beautiful place, the buildings being handsomely built of stone. The Abbey Church, or Cathedral, is well worth looking at, though inferior to Wells Cathedral. It was originally the church of an Abbey, from whence it is still called the Abbey Church. Bath, though a remarkable place for its beauty and antiquity, is chiefly famous for its natural hot springs, which have some important and highly useful medical qualities.

Bristol stands partly in Gloucestershire. It is a very ancient place, and was most likely founded in early British times. It has been a very important town for many centuries. The streets are generally narrow and the appearance of the city is not favourable. But the neighbourhood (as I have said already) makes up for the want of beauty in the city itself. The Cathedral has some beautiful parts, but it is not a fine building on the whole.

The ruins of Glastonbury Abbey are very remarkable from their standing probably on the very spot where the first church was erected in England. Some say that Joseph of Arimathea preached here; but without going quite so far back, we may be sure that Christianity was preached at this place at a very early period.

SOMERSETSHIRE

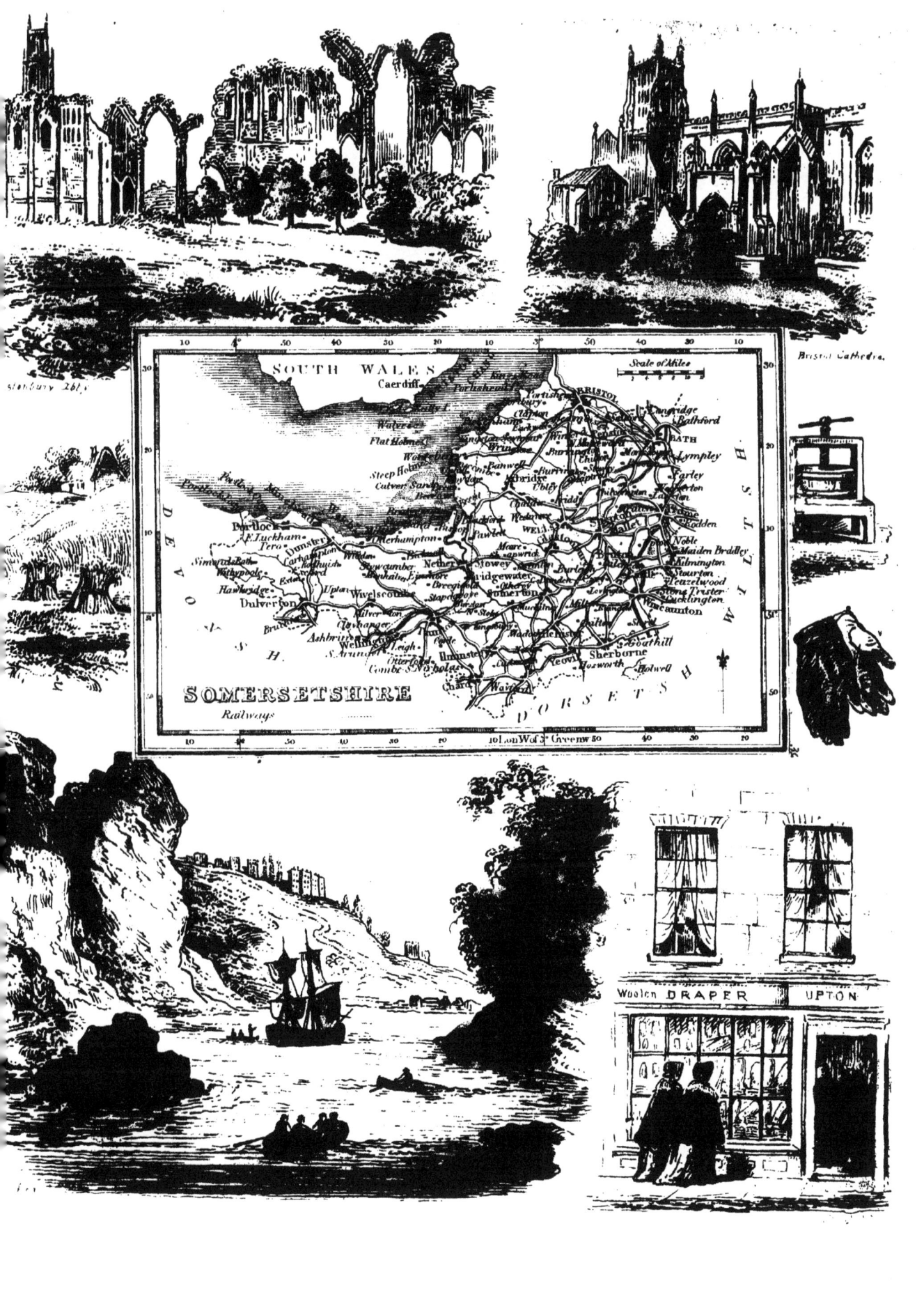

City of Oxford

Christ Church

Radcliffe Library

St Mary's Church

OXFORDSHIRE
Railways

Blenheim

OXFORDSHIRE.

Oxfordshire is an inland county, containing 162,000 people. A part of the river Thames, which is called the Isis, runs through it. The name of Oxford is said to have been given first to the part of the county in which the city now stands, because at that place there was a ford for oxen over the river Thames.

Oxford is one of the most beautiful cities in England. It stands almost upon an island, being nearly surrounded by the two rivers, the Isis and the Cherwell; and on all sides, at a little distance, there are pleasant hills, some of them covered with fine wood. But the great beauty of the city consists in the colleges, most of which are very handsome buildings, with fine gardens and avenues of trees attached to them. These colleges are parts of the University of Oxford, one of the most famous places of learning in the world.

A University is a place in which that knowledge is taught which concerns all men; and from

OXFORDSHIRE.

this it takes its name. It is not a place where merely law or medicine is taught, to make men lawyers or physicians; but a great part of the instruction which is given at a University, is in those subjects of which every man must learn something; only they are here studied more deeply than in common schools, in order that those who learn them should know how to teach others.

The University of Oxford is said to have been founded by king Alfred, and it is certain that it existed before the time of Edward the Confessor. The largest of the colleges is called Christ Church, and was founded by Cardinal Wolsey. It is close to the cathedral, which is a very ancient building, but not so beautiful as many other cathedrals. The college called University College is said to be the most ancient in Oxford. The University Church, which is dedicated to St. Mary, has a very beautiful spire, and is a handsome building.

Blenheim House, which is in this county, is a very fine place, which was given by Queen Anne to the great Duke of Marlborough, who gained so many battles during her reign.

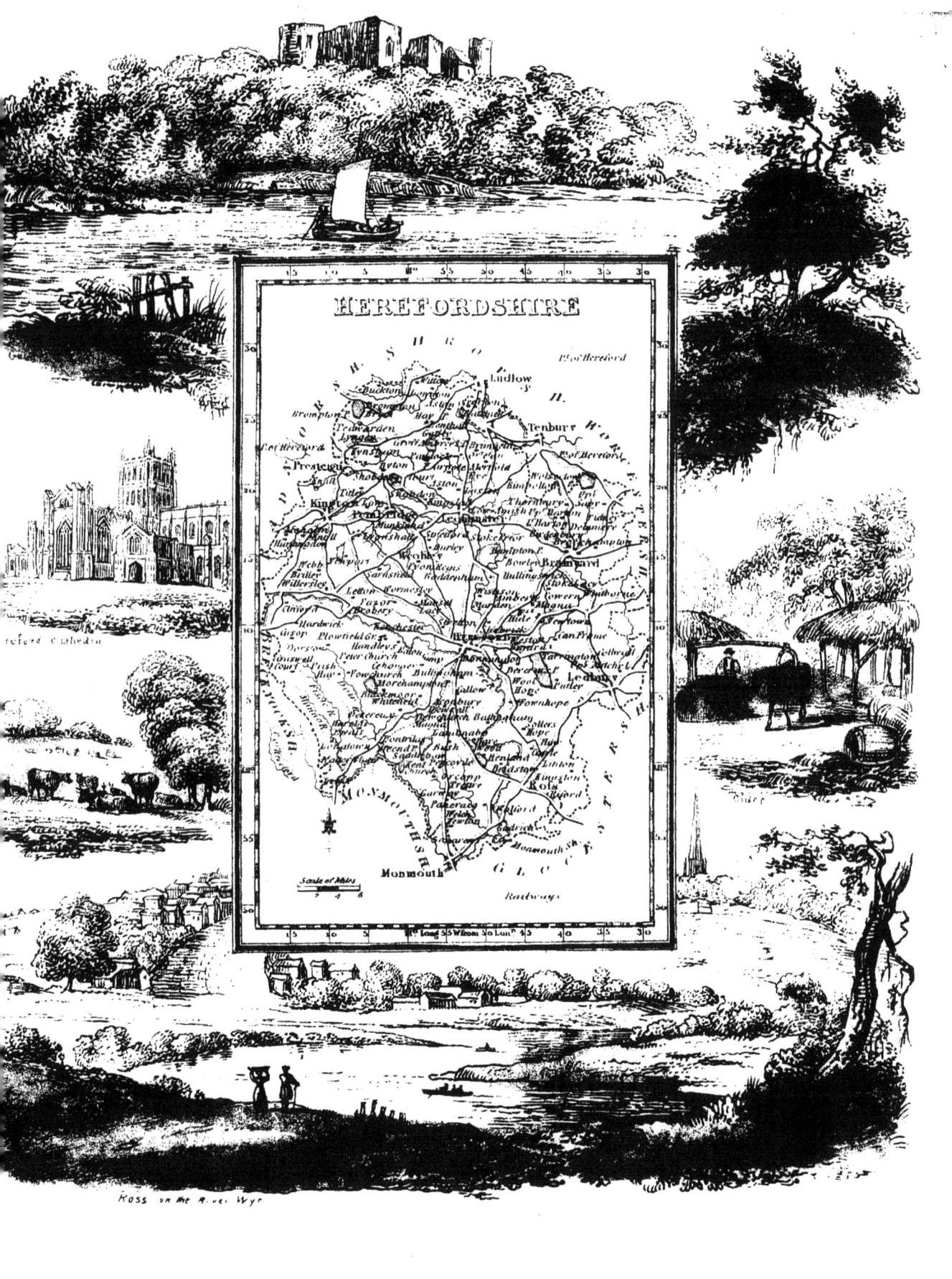

HEREFORDSHIRE

Ross on the River Wye

HEREFORDSHIRE.

HEREFORDSHIRE is an inland county on the borders of Wales, which contains 115,000 inhabitants. The river Wye runs through it. The capital is the city of Hereford.

The scenery of the banks of the river Wye is not so beautiful in its course through this county as in Monmouthshire, though it is very pleasing, and so is the whole county. The soil is fertile, and produces vast quantities of apples and hops. There is no county in England which produces such fine apples, and the cider which is made from them is very celebrated. The oxen and the sheep are also very fine.

Herefordshire was in ancient times the scene of many battles with the Welch. Along with Shropshire and Monmouthshire, it formed what was called " the Marches," or Border-land, which the Earls of March had to defend against the Welch. The castles of the Barons who lived in these counties,

HEREFORDSHIRE.

were very strong and numerous, as they were almost always at war. There are many ruins of these castles now remaining, and one of the most famous of them is Goodrich Castle, which stands upon a beautiful part of the river Wye.

Hereford is a pleasant city, and contains many old buildings. In the reign of Offa, it was the capital of the kingdom of Mercia, and the royal palace was at Sutton, which is about three miles distant. The cathedral was founded before the time of King Offa, but in his day it was built of wood, and was perhaps a very small building. It was rebuilt of stone twice before the Norman conquest; and in the reign of William, the present cathedral was built by Bishop Losing. It was a very fine old building till the year 1786, when a part of it fell down, and it has been since repaired in a very clumsy manner.

Ross is very beautifully situated on the Wye. It was in this town that "the Man of Ross" lived, respecting whom Pope has written a poem. His name was Kyrle.

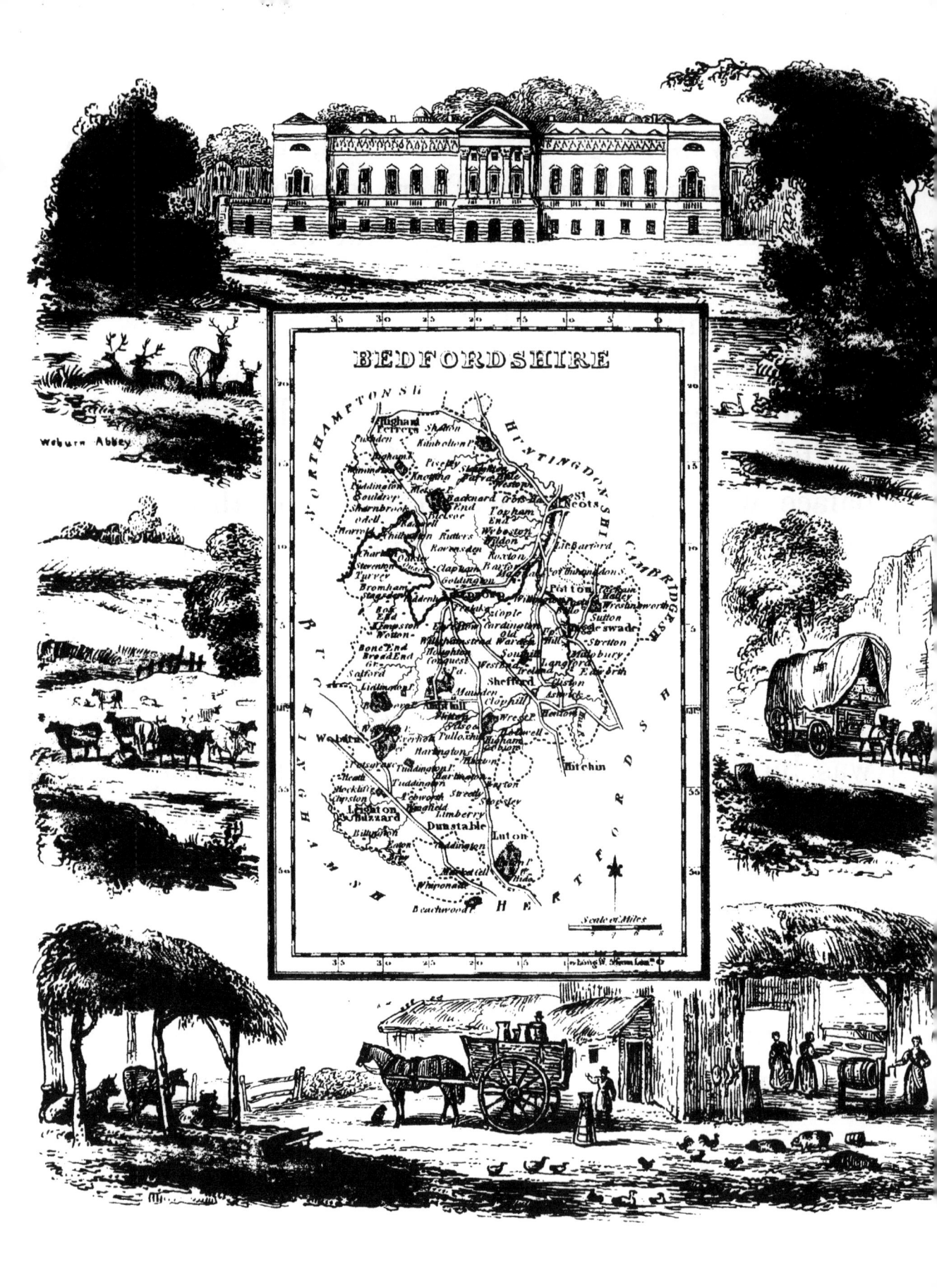

BEDFORDSHIRE

Woburn Abbey

BEDFORDSHIRE.

BEDFORDSHIRE is a small inland county, which contains 108,000 people. The capital is the town of Bedford.

The soil of Bedfordshire is very different in different parts; and though a great part of it is not naturally fertile, it is well cultivated, owing to the care which the Dukes of Bedford have taken to encourage agriculture. There is a large quantity of butter and of vegetables produced here, and sent to the London market.

Woburn Abbey is now the seat of the Duke of Bedford, and is the most interesting object in the county. It was formerly an abbey of the order of Monks called Cistercians, and was founded in the year 1145, by Hugh de Bolebec. When the Monks were turned out by King Henry VIII. the place was given to Lord Russell, who afterwards became the Earl of Bedford; and it has been held by his family ever since. A small part of the old building still remains, but the greater part of what is now standing is a very handsome new building.

BEDFORDSHIRE.

The park which surrounds it is very large and beautiful, abounding with fine trees. The gardens are extensive, and laid out with great taste. The abbey contains a great many paintings, a noble library, a gallery of sculpture, and a great collection of curious and beautiful things of different kinds.

There are the remains of an old British town not far from Dunstable, and near the same place is Toternhoe Castle, as it is called, which is either of British or Roman origin. It is a circular mount, surrounded by two circular banks.

Bedford is a very ancient town, which was probably standing when the Romans were in Britain. There was once a famous castle in the town, which was built in the reign of William Rufus. During the wars between the Kings and the Barons, in the reigns of John and Henry III. it was very often beseiged and taken; but at last it was destroyed by Henry, and has never been rebuilt.

It was at Bedford that John Bunyan, the author of "Pilgrim's Progress," lived, and the chapel in which he preached, and the prison in which he was confined, may still be seen. Bedford is a famous place for schools and charitable institutions.

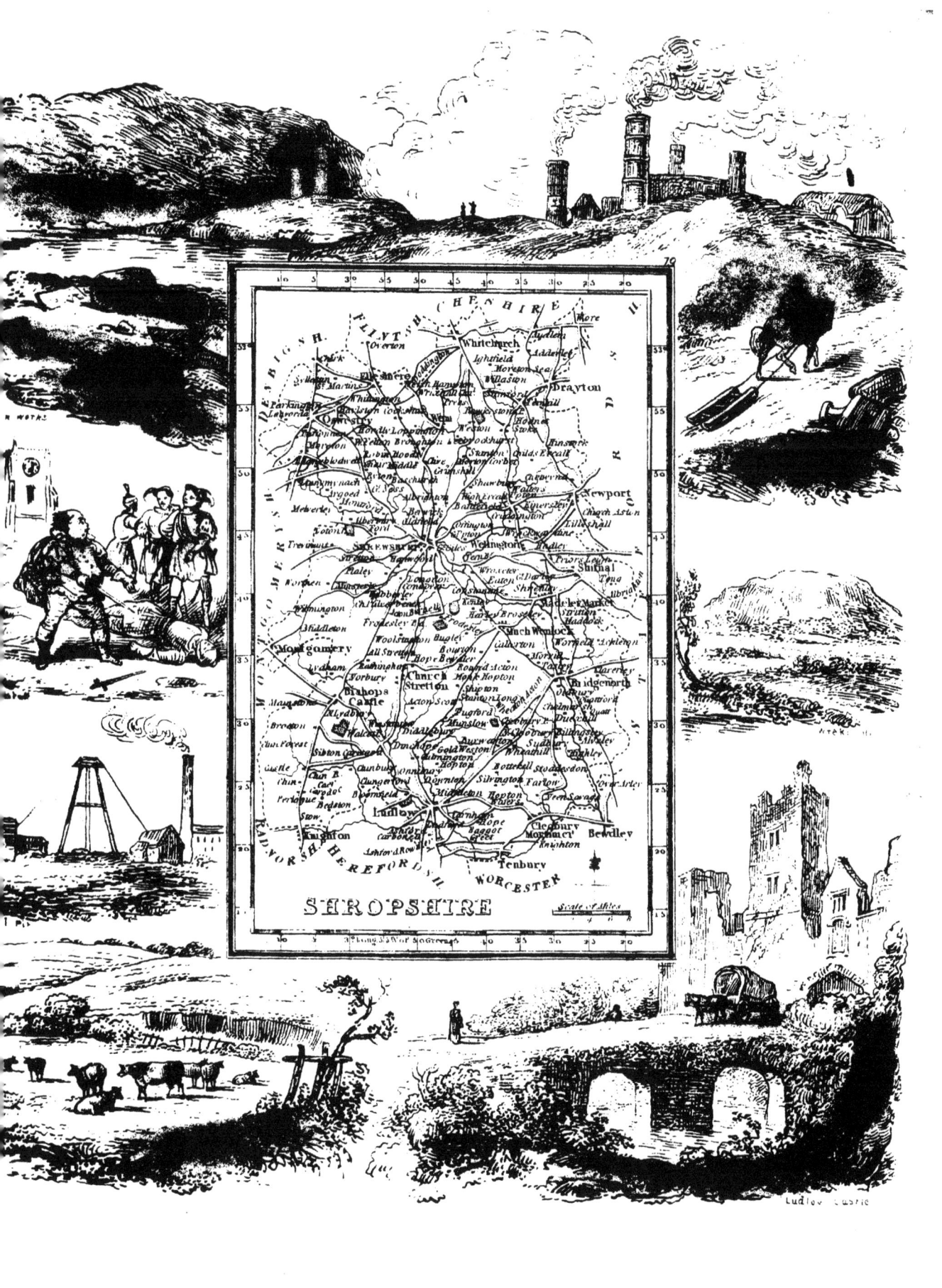

SHROPSHIRE

SHROPSHIRE.

Shropshire is an extensive county, but not so populous as most of the neighbouring English counties. It contains 240,000 inhabitants, is situated on the borders of Wales, and the river Severn runs through it. The capital is Shrewsbury.

A great part of the land of Shropshire is fertile, and produces abundance of grain. The scenery is pleasingly diversified by hill and dale. A very remarkable hill, 1320 feet in height, called "the Wrekin," stands not far from the town of Wellington. There are a large number of productive coal mines in the county, and great quantities of iron come from the neighbourhood of Colebrook Dale and other parts.

There is scarcely any county of which the history is more interesting than that of Shropshire. There are in it many traces of old British fortifications; and one of these, called Caer Caradoc, was an encampment of the army of the famous hero Caractacus, whose British name was Caradoc.

SHROPSHIRE.

There are also the remains of several Roman stations and roads. When the Saxons had conquered Britain, this county formed a chief part of the kingdom of Mercia; and here it is that traces may be seen of the fortification called Offa's Dyke, which King Offa formed to defend the country against the Welch.

The Earls of March, or of the Marches, as they were sometimes called, lived chiefly in Shropshire. They were appointed by the king, to defend the march or border-land against the Welch, who used frequently to make incursions into this county. There are some strong castles still remaining here, but the most famous is Ludlow Castle, where several kings have lived.

Shrewsbury is a fine old town, near which there was a famous battle fought, which is described in Shakspere's play of Henry IV. The Welch had been conquered by Edward I., but they submitted to the English very unwillingly. In the time of Henry IV. a man, named Owen Glendwyr, who was descended from the ancient Kings of Wales, stirred them up to rebel, but they were overcome in this battle.

STAFFORDSHIRE.

Staffordshire is an inland county. It is very populous, and contains 510,000 people. The capitals are the city of Lichfield and the town of Stafford.

Some parts of this county are well wooded, and contain some fine estates. But it is not in general fertile, and is more remarkable for what it contains underground than above. There are many coal and iron mines; and in the neighbourhood of Newcastle-under-Lyne are the most extensive manufactories in the world of china and other earthenware. The towns of Burslem, Hanley, Stoke, and their neighbourhoods, containing several small towns and villages, are called "the Potteries." The North part of the county contains fine beds of clay, out of which the pottery is made; while the South part contains great quantities of iron. Plenty of coal is to be found almost every where; and it is used in the North for baking the earthenware, and in the South for working the iron. The town of Wolverhampton, and the places round it, are very famous for their iron trade.

Tamworth is a very ancient town, where some of the Kings of Mercia resided in the time of the Saxon Heptarchy. There is a very ancient castle overlooking the town.

Dudley is a very interesting town, which was founded by Dodo, a Saxon prince, about the year 700. The castle was a very strong place, and the ruins now form a beautiful object at the top of a tall hill. Under the castle there is a curious stone quarry, from which limestone is obtained for the use of the iron works which are near. It is in the form of a long passage or tunnel, more than a mile in length, and thirteen feet high. The town is supported chiefly by the trade in iron goods.

Lichfield is a very pleasant city, and has a very beautiful cathedral, which was much injured during the civil wars, but was restored by the excellent Bishop Hackett, chiefly at his own expense. It contains a monument to two children, by Sir Francis Chantry, which is said to be one of the finest in England.

STAFFORDSHIRE

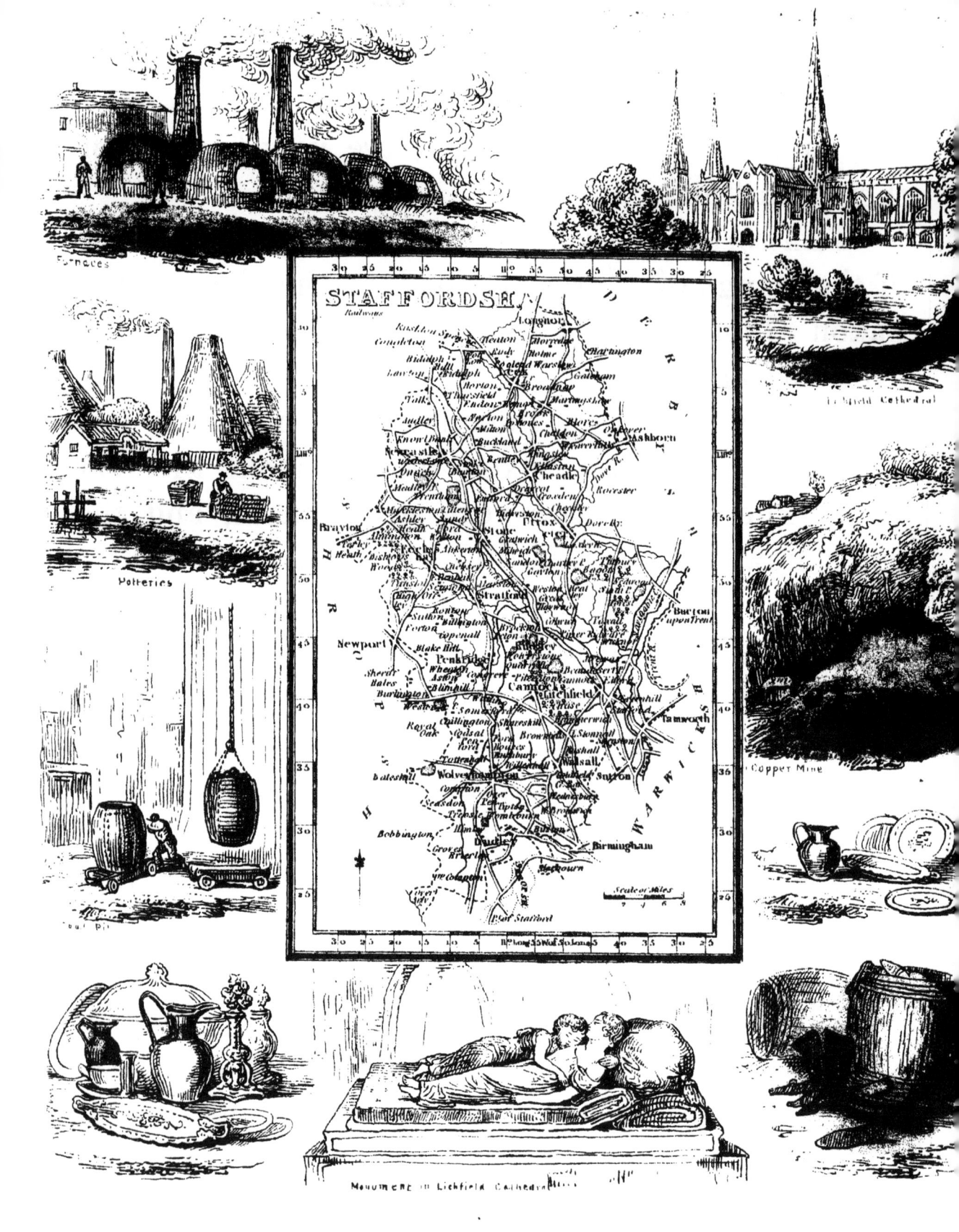

WARWICKSHIRE.

This is an inland county, and very populous, containing 402,000 inhabitants. The largest place in the county is Birmingham, of which the population is 140,000; but the capital is Warwick.

Warwickshire is a fine county, with plenty of wood and rich pasture. It contains a great many interesting places.

Warwick is a handsome and ancient town; but its great ornament is the castle, in which the Earl of Warwick now lives. It was a royal castle in the time of Edward the Confessor, but having been destroyed, it was rebuilt by Thomas Beauchamp, Earl of Warwick, who fought bravely in the battles of Cressy and Poictiers, when the Black Prince so distinguished himself. It has been kept in repair exactly in the style in which it was first built, and is now the finest specimen of a Baronial Castle in England

Kenilworth is another noble castle in this

WARWICKSHIRE.

county, but it is now in ruins. It was here that the famous John of Gaunt, Duke of Lancaster, lived; and, in later times, the Earl of Leicester entertained Queen Elizabeth in a very magnificent style.

Coventry is a large and very ancient town, with some fine churches. It is famous for the manufacture of silk goods and watches.

Birmingham is the most celebrated place in the world for the manufacture of iron, brass and plated articles. It is a very large town, with some fine buildings in it. The town hall is a noble specimen of architecture, and the Grammar School and the market place are built in excellent style. But it is not an agreeable place, from the smoke of the forges and furnaces which abound in it.

But the most interesting place in the county is Stratford-upon-Avon, the native place of Shakspere, the greatest poet that ever lived. The house in which he was born is still standing; and his tomb, with a bust of him, is to be seen in the Church.

Warwick Castle

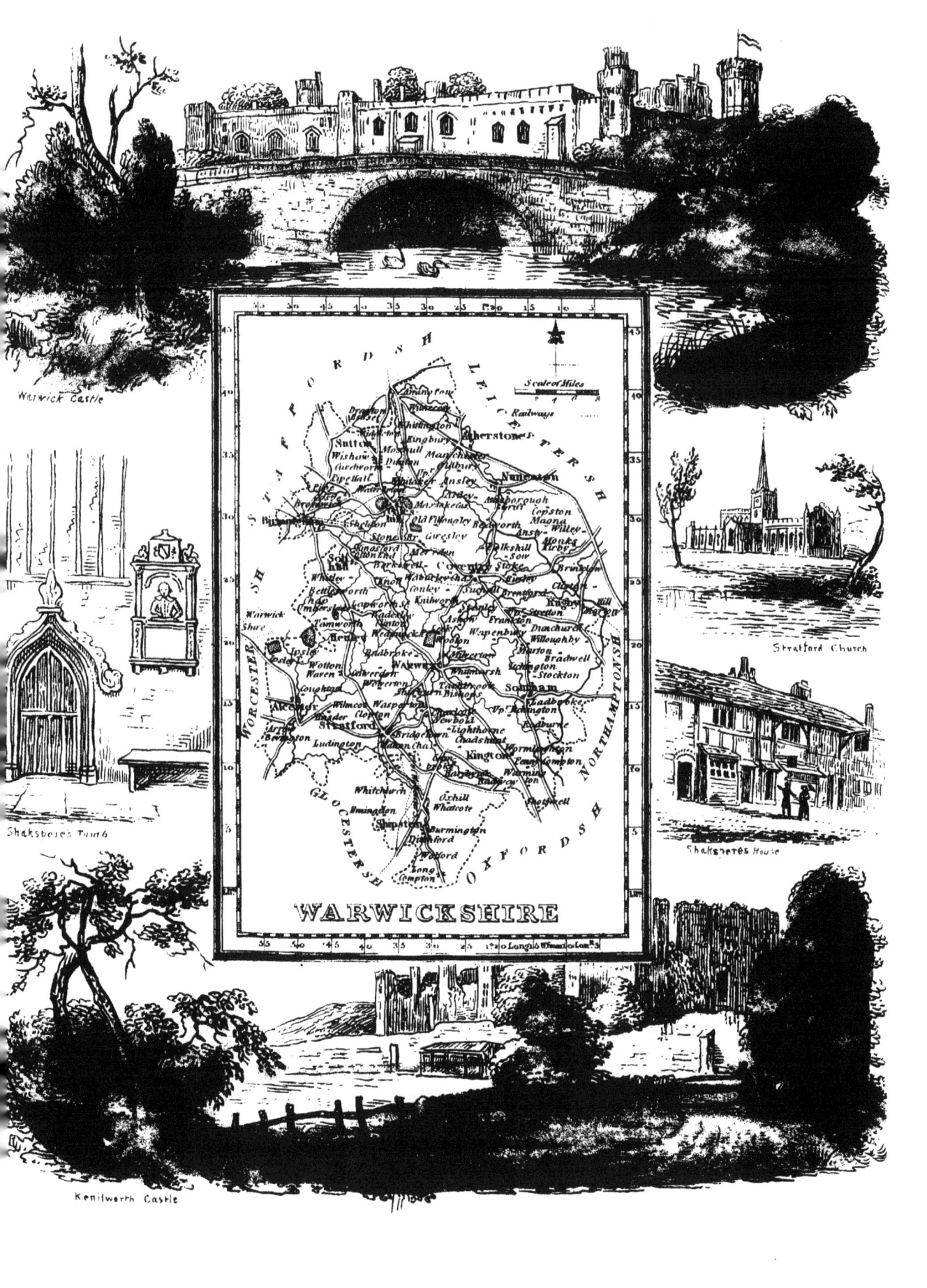

Shakspere's Tomb

Kenilworth Castle

WARWICKSHIRE

Stratford Church

Shakspere's House

MONMOUTHSHIRE.

British Kings, Uther Pendragon and Arthur are said to have lived. Chepstow was founded when the Romans were here, and now contains the ruins of a very large and strong castle.

In the times of the Saxon Heptarchy, and for a long time afterwards, the English and the Welch were always fighting for Monmouthshire, and sometimes one nation held it, and sometimes the other. It was hardly determined to be a part of England till the reign of Charles II.

The ruins of Tintern Abbey are considered to be the most beautiful ruins in England. The Abbey was founded in 1131, by Walter de Clare, and was inhabited by Cistercian Monks. The church of the Abbey was built by the Earl of Norfolk, in the year 1268. When the Monasteries were put down by Henry VIII. the Abbey was given to the Earl of Worcester, but at present it belongs to the Duke of Beaufort.

The ruins of Llanthony Abbey are now almost destroyed, but what remain are very interesting. The style of architecture belongs to an earlier age than that of Tintern, and the buildings were most likely erected a hundred years before.

MONMOUTHSHIRE

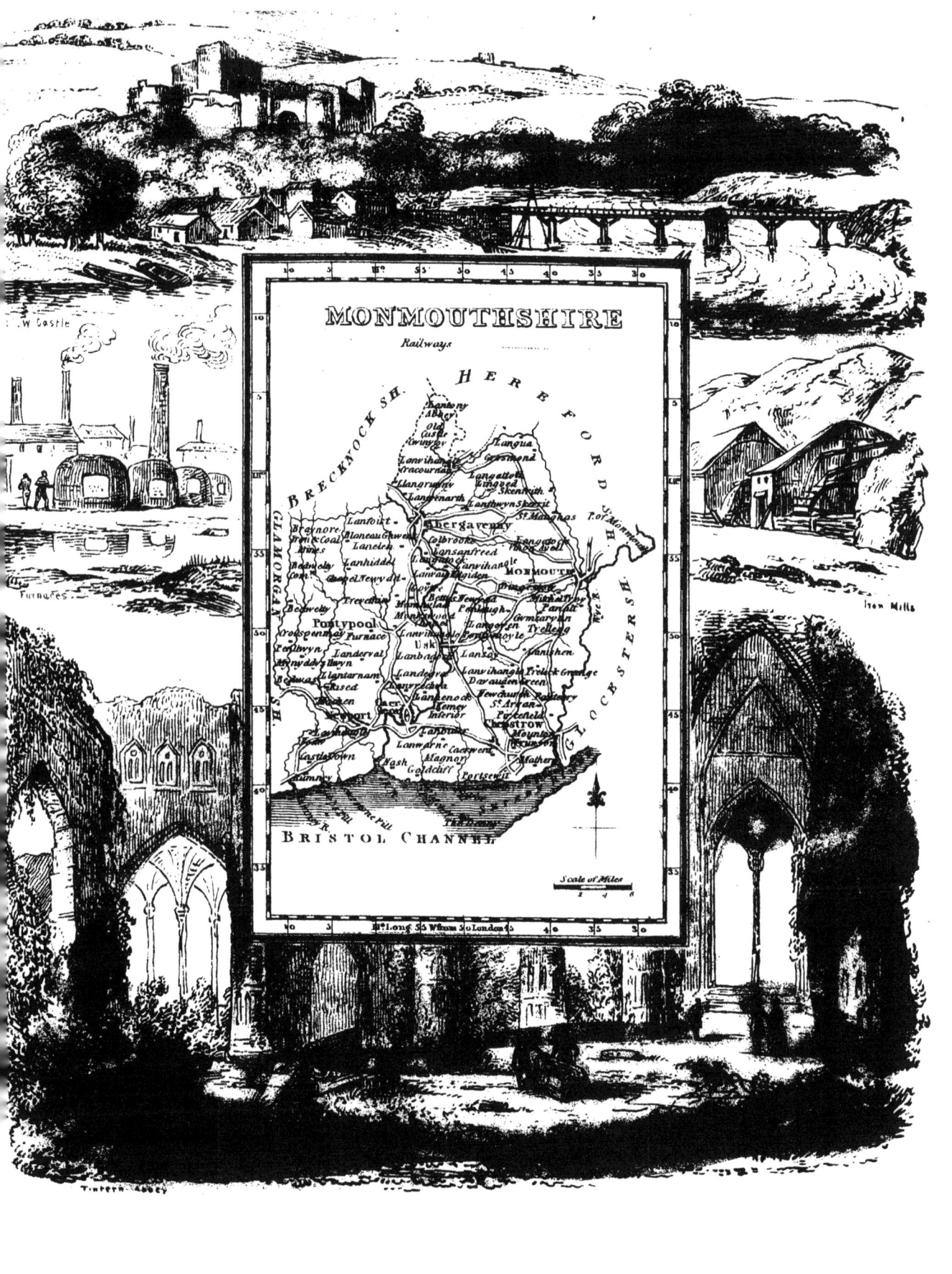

WORCESTERSHIRE.

WORCESTERSHIRE is a very pleasant county. The river Severn runs through it, and it contains 233,000 inhabitants. The capital is the city of Worcester.

The land of this county is generally fertile, and produces plenty of corn of all kinds; but it is more famous for trees and fruit, especially apples and pears. A very large quantity of salt is made from the salt springs which rise at Droitwich. The part called the Vale of Evesham is very beautiful, and so is the scenery of the Malvern Hills.

Worcester is a fine city, with wide and well-built streets. The cathedral was founded by Ethelred, King of Mercia, one of the states of the Saxon Heptarchy in which Worcester stood; but it has been rebuilt several times since his days. The present structure was built about five hundred years ago. It contains the tombs of King John and of his nephew Prince Arthur, whom, it is said, he cruelly murdered, because the prince had a claim

WORCESTERSHIRE.

to the throne of England which interfered with his own. These tombs originally stood in the old building.

There was a great battle fought at Worcester, between Oliver Cromwell and the Scotch friends of Charles II., after which Charles was obliged to fly from the country. There are a great many gloves made at Worcester, and a fine sort of China-ware. The town of Kidderminster is famous for the manufacture of carpets, and there is one kind of carpet which takes its name from the town.

Evesham is a very interesting town, and beautifully situated. It contains the ruins of an abbey, which was founded in the year 709. The part which remains is called the Abbot's Tower, having been built by one of the abbots, named Clement Lichfield, in the time of Henry VI. It was at Evesham that Prince Edward, afterwards King Edward I., conquered the celebrated Simon de Montfort, Earl of Leicester, who had rebelled against King Henry III. Simon de Montfort was a Frenchman, who was the author of the plan of the English House of Commons.

Malvern

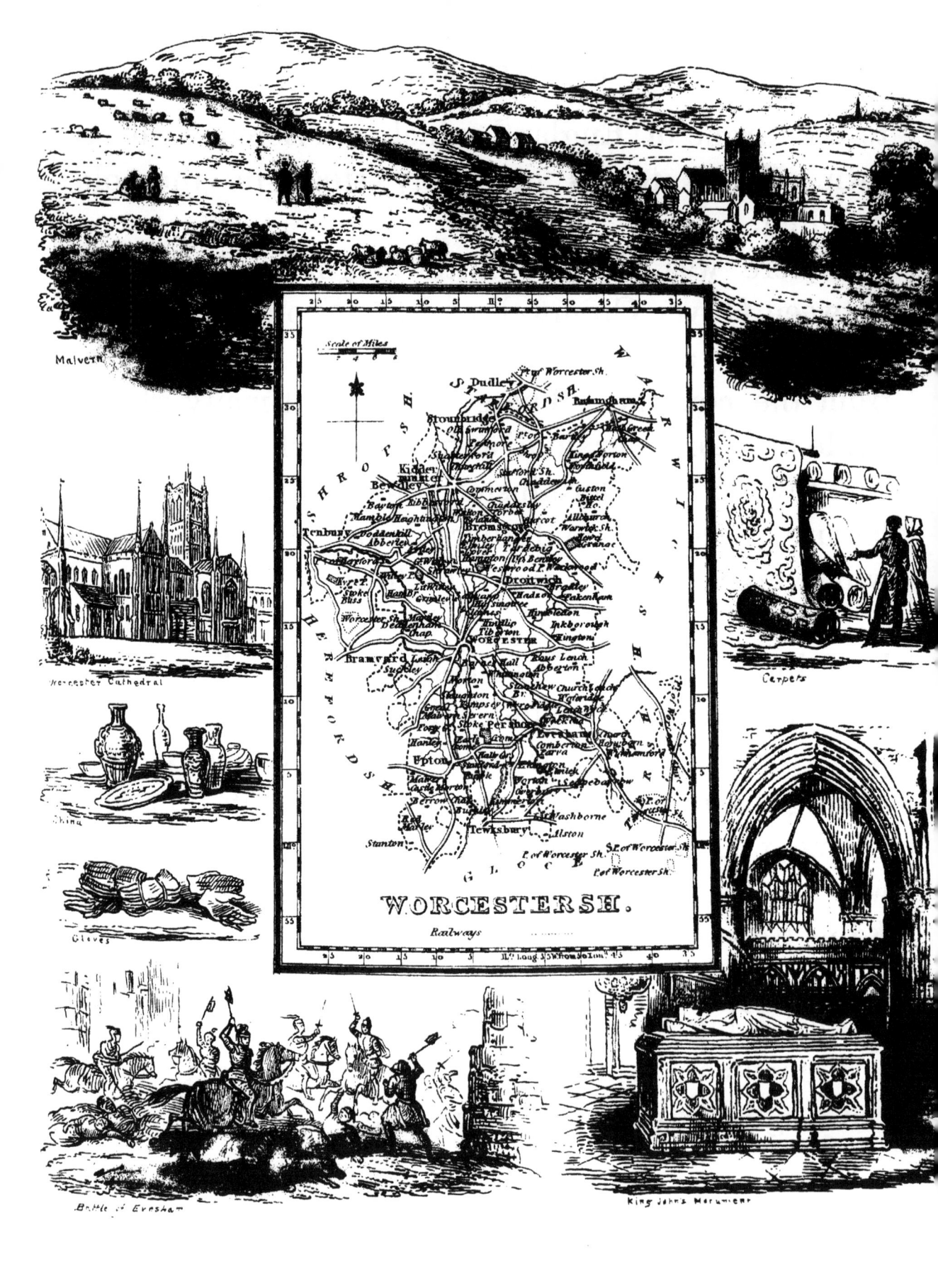

Worcester Cathedral

China

Gloves

Battle of Evesham

WORCESTERSH.
Railways

Carpets

King John's Monument

CAMBRIDGESH.
Railways
LINCOLNSH
NORFOLK
SUFFOLK
HUNTINGDONSH
BEDFORDS
HERTFORDSH
ESSEX
Wisbeach
Newmarket
CAMBRIDGE
Caxton
Royston
Linton
Soham
Scale of Miles
NEWTON
King's College
Gate of Trinity College
Christ College

CAMBRIDGESHIRE.

Cambridgeshire is an inland county, with a population of 164,000. The chief places are the town of Cambridge and the city of Ely.

The land of this county is generally very flat, but the greater part is fertile, and produces plenty of corn and fine grass. There is very little wood in the county, and most of the scenery is therefore very dull and uninteresting.

Cambridge is a disagreeable town. It takes its name from a bridge over the river Cam, which flows through it. The town was an important place at the time of the conquest, and king Richard II. held a parliament here.

The University of Cambridge is a very celebrated place of learning. The colleges which belong to it do not improve the appearance of the town so much as those of Oxford, because they do not stand in such good situations. The largest of them is Trinity College. The buildings of several are very fine, but

CAMBRIDGESHIRE.

the most handsome of all is King's College, the Chapel of which is the most beautiful structure of its kind in England. It was built by King Henry VI., and to him the College owes its name.

The University is very old, and it is said by some to be older than Oxford; but this is not very likely.

The city of Ely is supposed to have had its name from the great number of eels which are produced in the neighbourhood. The Cathedral is a noble building, though it was built piecemeal. The oldest portion was erected in the reign of William Rufus, and the other parts at various times down to 1534, so that it was more than four hundred years in building. The interior is remarkably beautiful, and contains some very fine carving in wood. A great monastery, founded in the seventh century by Anna, the Queen of East Anglia, once stood where the Cathedral now is.

Cambridgeshire was in ancient times a part of the land of the Iceni, the British tribe, of which Boadicea was Queen, who fought so bravely against the Romans, and was at last conquered by them with great difficulty. Many Roman remains are found in the county.

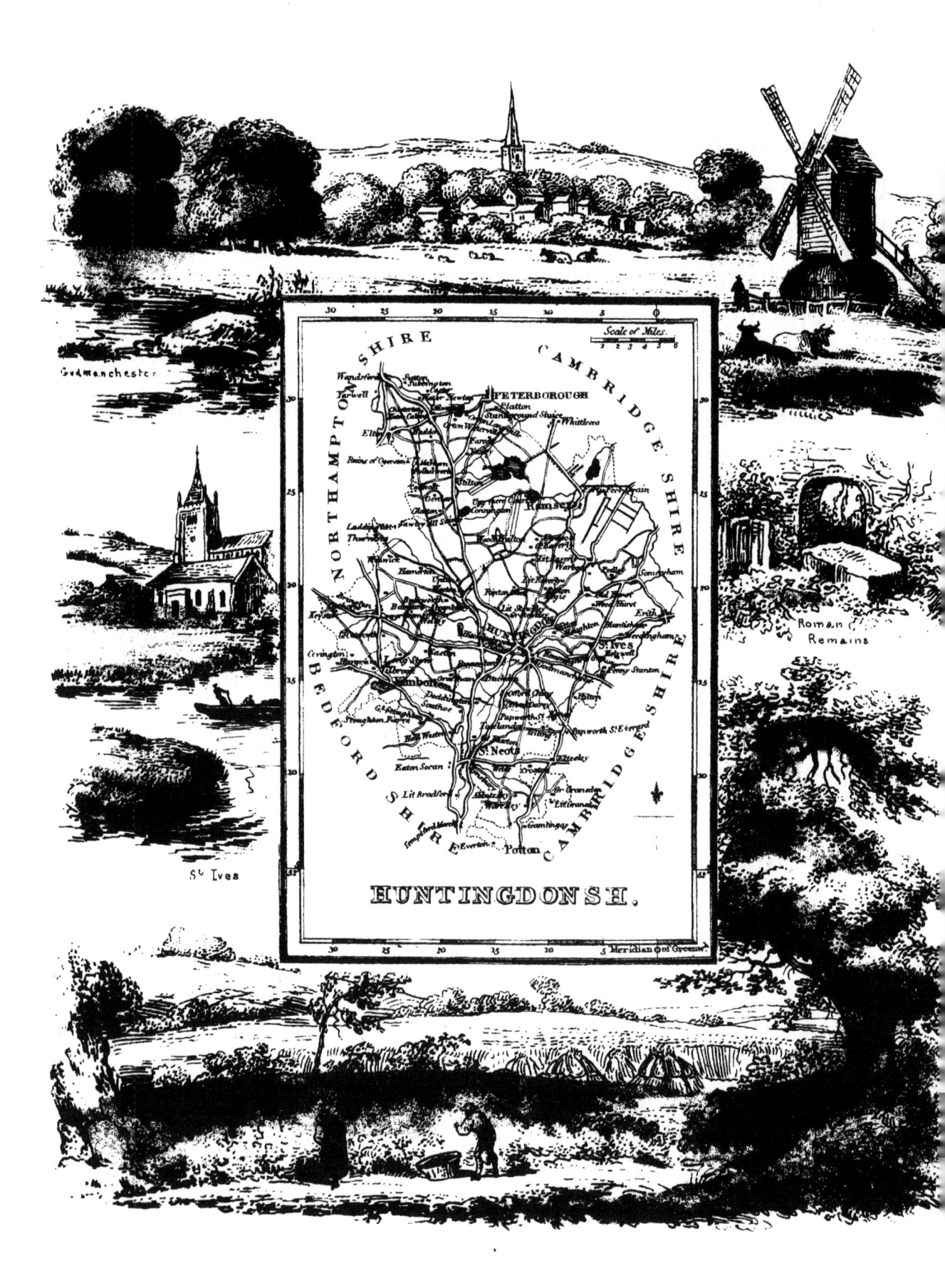

HUNTINGDONSH.

HUNTINGDONSHIRE.

This is a small inland county, containing 59,000 inhabitants. Its capital is the town of Huntingdon.

A great part of the county is destitute of springs, and is supplied with water by pools or small lakes. The largest of these are called Meres, like the lakes of Cumberland, and are in the North corner of the county. They are called Whittlesea-mere, Ramsey-mere, and Ugg-mere. They contain plenty of fish, and are frequented by many water fowl.

Huntingdonshire is not very fertile; but it produces a large quantity of barley and of mustard. There are but few trees, and they are generally small, though in the reign of King Henry II. the whole county was a forest. The trees were cut down chiefly by Henry II. and Edward I.

Huntingdon was once a much larger place than it is at present, and is said to have contained fifteen churches, though there are now but two. It is united with a town or village called Godmanchester,

HUNTINGDONSHIRE.

which was founded in Roman times. There are the remains of an old castle at Huntingdon, which was built by one of the Saxon Kings, and was afterwards given by King Stephen to David, Earl of Huntingdon and King of Scotland, who was a vassal of the English King. Oliver Cromwell was born at this town.

At Kimbolton there is a castle, in which the family of the Dukes of Manchester, whose name was Montague, lived for several ages. Queen Catharine of Aragon, after she was divorced from Henry VIII., lived and died in this castle, and was buried in Peterborough Cathedral.

St. Ives is an old town, which was called by the early Saxons "Slepe." It took its present name from St. Ivo, a Persian missionary, who came to England about the year 600, and was buried here. The church is an interesting building, having some parts very old and others quite new.

Stilton, which has given its name to Stilton cheese, is in this county; but most of the cheese which goes by the name of Stilton, is made in Leicestershire.

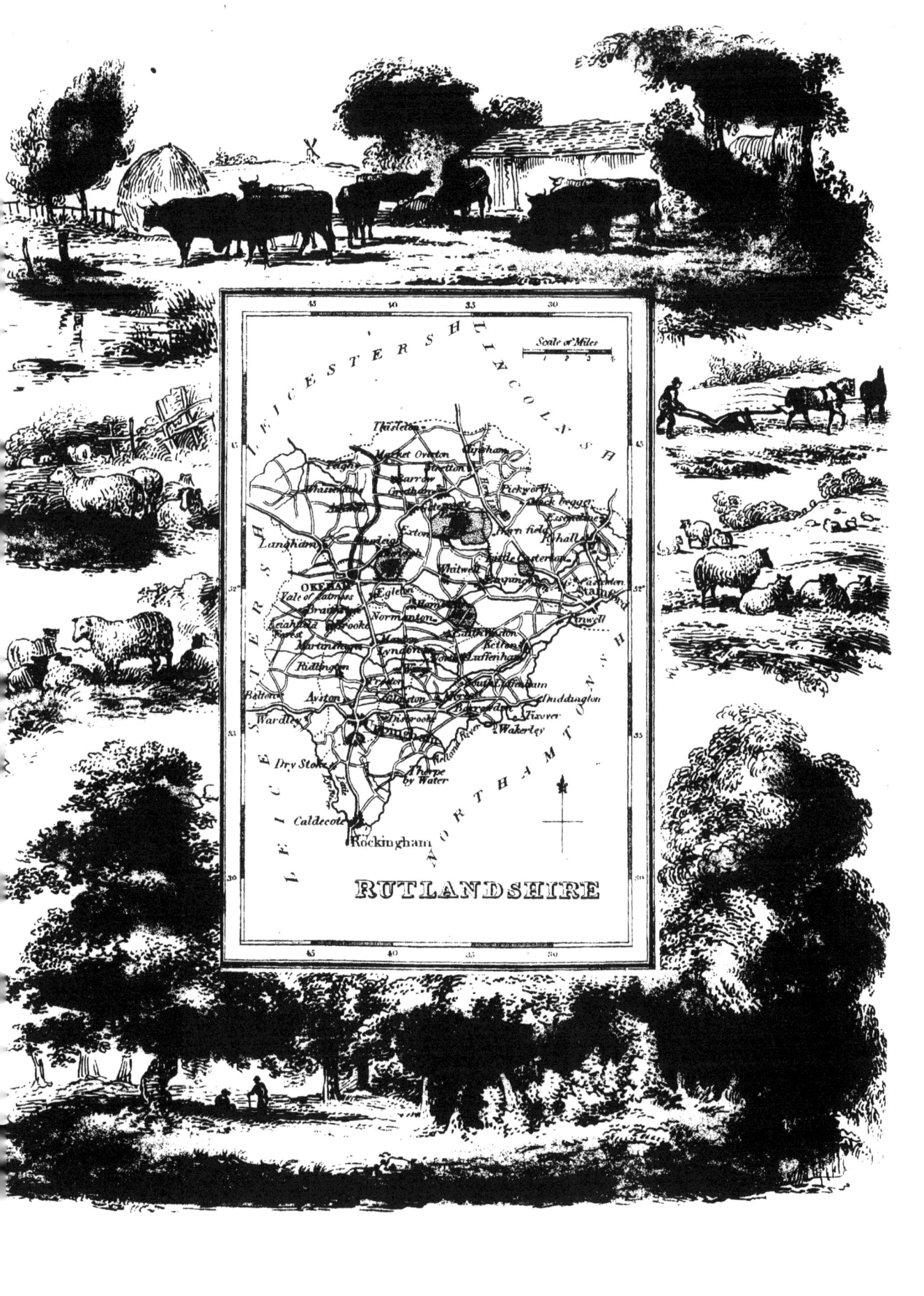

RUTLANDSHIRE

RUTLANDSHIRE.

This is the smallest of the English counties, being only nineteen miles long, and fourteen miles wide. The population is 21,000. Middlesex, which is the next in size, is nearly twice as large as Rutland, and contains more than seventy times as many inhabitants; and Yorkshire, which is the largest county, is forty times as large. The chief town in Rutland is Oakham, which contains only 2,500 people, and is not larger than many villages.

The land of Rutland is well cultivated, and one half of it produces very fine pasture, and the rest corn of all kinds and wood. The sheep and oxen are excellent, the sheep being of the same kind as those of Leicestershire. There are some extensive woods, from which fine oak and ash timber is obtained. Much of the land which was once a forest is now laid out in fine parks, of which there are a great many in Rutland, for the size of the county.

There was formerly an ancient castle at Oakham, built in the reign of Henry II. It was inhabited by

RUTLANDSHIRE.

Richard, the king of the Romans, the brother of Henry III., by Thomas Cromwell, Earl of Essex, the wicked Duke of Buckingham in the time of Charles II., and many other famous persons. The Town Hall, in which the assizes are held, is almost the only remaining part of the castle. There are on the gate a number of horse-shoes, which were placed there according to a strange custom. The Lord of the Castle had authority to demand from every Peer who passed through his lands, for the first time, a shoe from one of his horses, or else a sum of money to buy one. These horse-shoes were all nailed upon the gate and walls of the outer court of the Castle. Some of them are gilt and stamped with the giver's name. There is one shoe that was given by Queen Elizabeth and another by King George IV.

At Hornfield, in this county, the battle of Lose-coat-field was fought by King Edward IV., against some rebels, who had come out of Lincolnshire, in the year 1468. The battle had its name of Lose-coat-field, because the rebels who ran away, threw off their coats that they might run the faster.

Norwich Cathedral

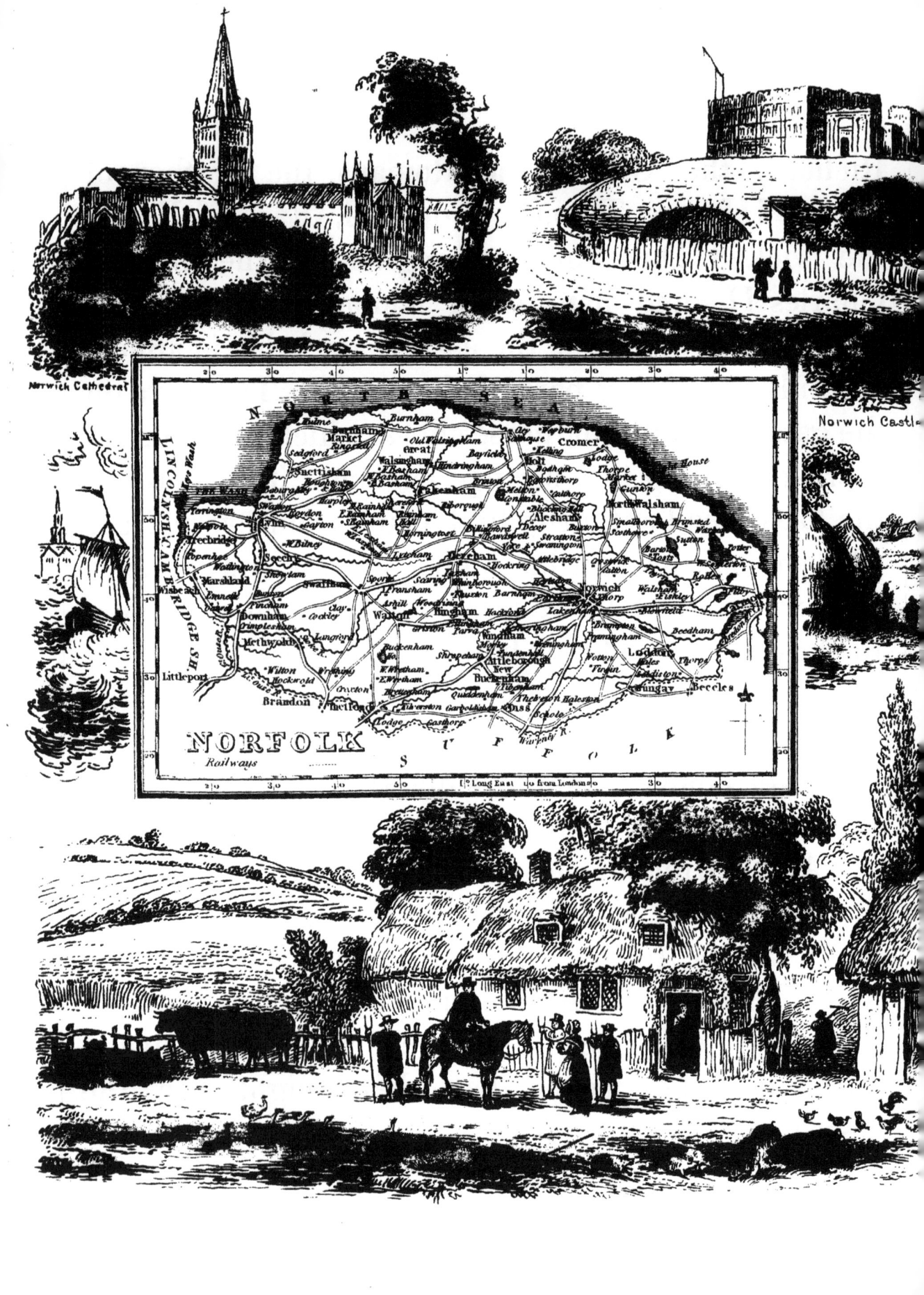

Norwich Castle

NORFOLK
Railways

NORFOLK.

This county contains 413,000 people. It is called Norfolk, or North-folk, because when the body of Saxons which took possession of the East part of England landed, they separated into two parties, one of which was called Norfolk and the other South-folk, or Suffolk. The capital of Norfolk is the city of Norwich.

The land of this county is flat, but fertile, and produces much corn and grass. There is no part of England in which agriculture has been more successfully encouraged.

Norwich is a large city, containing 62,000 inhabitants, and is famous for the manufacture of silk and stuff. It was a considerable place in the time of the Saxons; and in the reign of Edward the Confessor it was the third city in the kingdom; London and York only being larger. The castle was once a royal residence, and was very strongly fortified. A portion of it has lately been restored.

The Cathedral was founded about thirty years after the conquest by Bishop Losing, in whose time the see was removed from Thetford to Norwich. It

NORFOLK.

is not so large nor so much decorated as some of our cathedrals, but still it is a fine building, and has a very graceful spire.

Great Yarmouth stands at the mouth of the river Yare. It is a flourishing sea port, and is a great place for fishing. It is called Great Yarmouth to distinguish it from Yarmouth, in the Isle of Wight. The herrings which are caught off the coast of Norfolk are called Yarmouth herrings, and are some of the finest in the world. It is supposed that this arises from the nature of the sea-weed on which the fish feed, for all the herrings we get in this country come in one great shoal at a certain season of the year from the North Seas. When they come to Scotland, they divide into two parties, one of which takes the East coast of Great Britain and the other the West.

There are many interesting ruins in Norfolk, of which those best worth notice are the Abbeys of Thetford, Walsingham and Wymondham, and Binham Priory. In the time of the Saxon Heptarchy, the county was included with Suffolk and Cambridgeshire in the powerful kingdom of East Anglia.

LINCOLNSHIRE.

This is the second in size of the English counties, being next to Yorkshire in extent. It is seventy-six miles long and fifty-two miles wide, and contains 362,000 inhabitants. The capital is the city of Lincoln.

A great part of Lincolnshire is very flat, and you may travel in it for miles without seeing a hill. The flat part is called "the Fens." The soil is in some places unproductive, but in others it is very rich and produces some of the best pasture in England. The farmers who live in the Fens keep a great number of geese, and most of the quills which we use come from Lincolnshire.

Lincoln is a very ancient city, which was founded by the ancient Britons; and at the time of the Norman conquest, it was one of the most important places in England. It contains a gate, which was built by the Romans, and also a fine tesselated pavement, which is close to the Cathedral. Coins of the Emperors Nero, Vespasian and Julian have been

LINCOLNSHIRE.

found in considerable numbers. Carausius, who tried to make himself the Sovereign of Britain while it was under the Romans, is said to have lived at Lincoln for some time. One of the great Roman roads ran through Lincoln, and it may still be traced reaching in a straight line from the city to the river Humber.

The Cathedral is the most beautiful of the English Cathedrals except York Minster. It stands upon a very steep hill, overlooking the city; and the situation is as fine as the building. It may be seen at the distance of several miles.

There is a famous bell in the Cathedral, called the Tom of Lincoln, which weighs five tons. It is the third bell in England, the largest being the Mighty Tom of Oxford, which weighs seven tons and a half; and the second, the Great Tom of Exeter, which is six tons. The Tom of Lincoln was cracked a few years ago, and the present bell was cast in the year 1835.

Lincolnshire is celebrated for its fine churches, and two of the finest are at Boston and Louth; the former has a beautiful tower, and the latter a graceful steeple.

Boston Church & Iron Bridge

LINCOLNSHIRE

LEICESTERSHIRE.

Leicestershire is an inland county, containing 215,000 inhabitants. The capital is the town of Leicester.

There is very little wood in this county, but the pasture is remarkably rich. The sheep which are bred here are very celebrated, and have fine long wool. It is of their skins that the best sheep-skin mats are made; and the wool is some of the best in the world, for the manufacture of blankets and carpets, from its great length. The cows are also very fine, and most of them have long horns. The part of the county in which Melton Mowbray stands, is very famous for fox hunting and all sorts of sporting; for it not only contains great quantities of game, but the country is a good one to ride over.

Leicester is a large town, containing 50,000 people. It is principally supported, like Nottingham, by the manufacture of stockings. The name is

LEICESTERSHIRE.

said to be derived from the famous King Lear, the son of Bladud; and it was probably first called Lear-chester by the Romans, and this became changed into Leicester. You may read of how King Lear was deprived of his kingdom by his two wicked daughters, and how he and his one good daughter died in trying to recover their rights, in Shakspere's play of King Lear.

There is but little remaining now of the castle of Leicester, which was once a very strong place. It was held by the friends of Robert, Duke of Normandy, the son of the Conqueror; and was taken from them and destroyed by William Rufus. It was soon rebuilt, and belonged for some time to the Dukes of Lancaster; and when the Kings of the house of Lancaster were reigning, several of them lived in it. In the reign of Charles I. it fell to ruin, and has never been restored.

There is a piece of an old wall in Leicester, called the Jewry wall, which was built by the Romans. There have been found many other Roman remains in the county, particularly at Market Harborough.

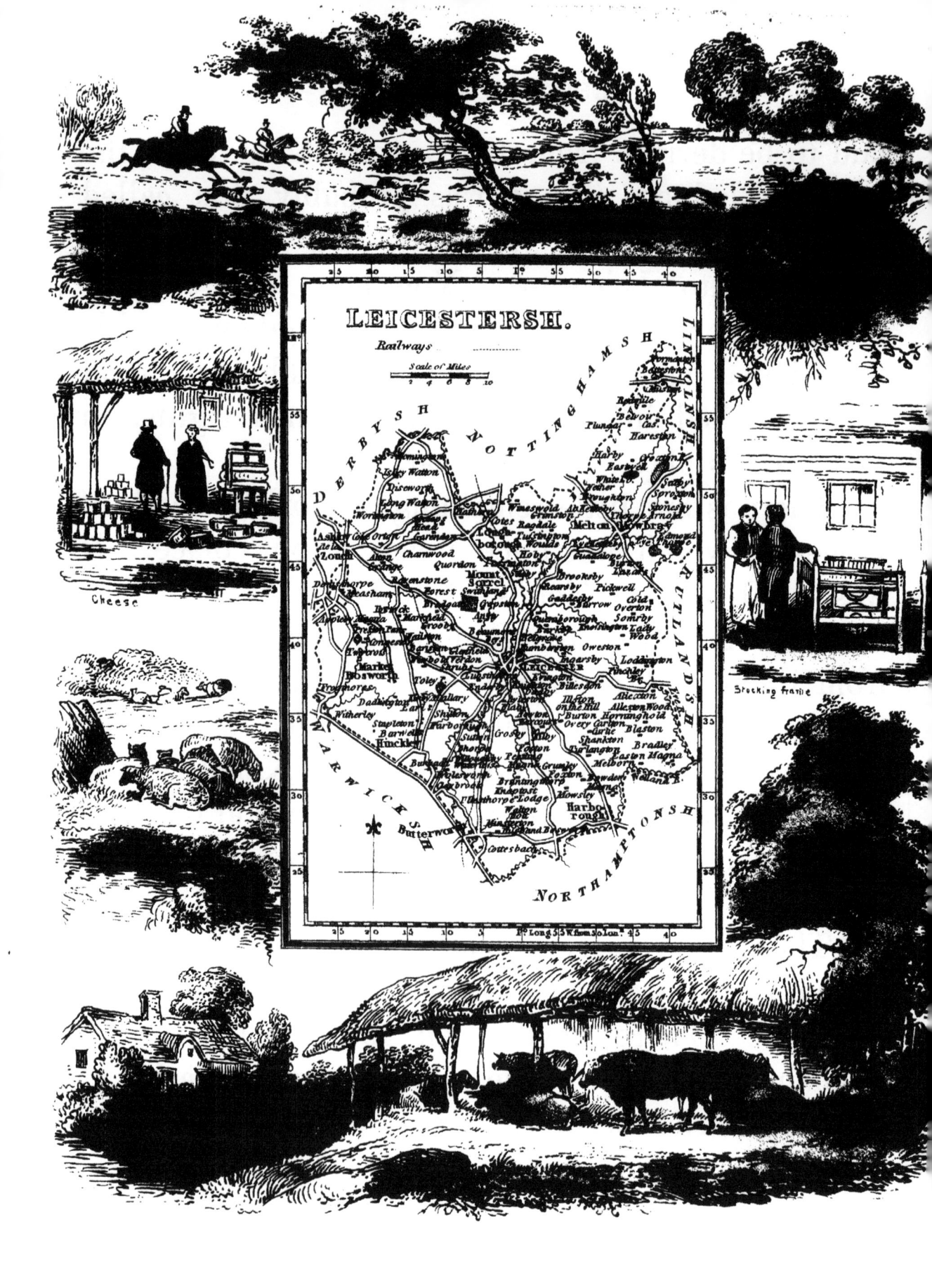

LEICESTERSH.

Railways ....
Scale of Miles

Cheese

Stocking frame

NOTTINGHAMSHIRE.

Nottinghamshire is an inland county, containing 250,000 inhabitants. The capital is the town of Nottingham.

There is a pleasant mixture of hills and vales in Nottinghamshire, though there are no very high hills. In former times a great part of the county was covered by forests, but these have now been cleared away, and most of the wood remaining is in parks, of which there are a great number. Coal is obtained in several parts. Near Nottingham there are some very curious caverns dug out of the sandstone, on which the town stands. These are supposed to have been the habitations of some of the first inhabitants of this part of the country.

The town of Nottingham is a large place, with a population of 53,000. It is famous for the manufacture of stockings. The castle, which stands on a rock, is not now a fine building, but it was very different in ancient times. It was given by

NOTTINGHAMSHIRE.

William the Conqueror to his son William Peverel, and was the scene of a great many strange events. The celebrated Colonel Hutchinson was the governor of this castle in the time of Charles I.

At Southwell there is a very fine Collegiate Church, which was most likely built in the reign of William I. A Collegiate Church is one in which there are a Dean and Canons, as there are in a Cathedral, but which is not a Bishop's see.

There have been some very interesting Roman remains discovered at Mansfield and Newark. Newstead Abbey is a very beautiful building, which was founded by Henry II., and was inhabited by Cistercian Monks. Of late it has become celebrated as the residence of the poet Lord Byron. Sherwood Forest was the place in which Robin Hood lived. This famous man was a member of a good family, and some say that he was related to the Earls of Huntingdon. He lived the life of an outlaw and a robber, though he was always kind to the poor. He died in 1247, and was buried at Kirklees, in Yorkshire, where his tomb is still to be seen.

NOTTINGHAMSH.

Newstead Abbey

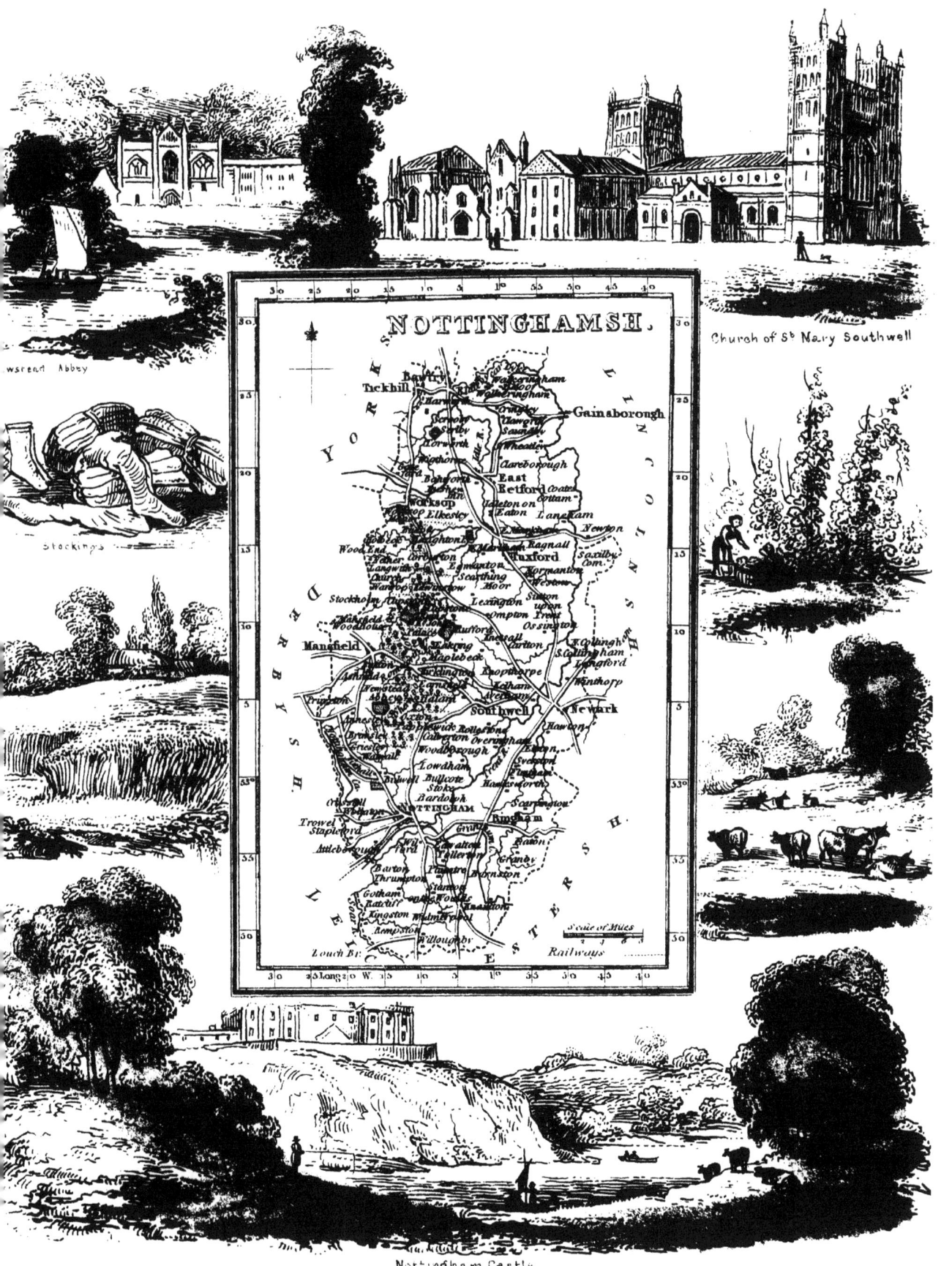

Stockings

Church of St Mary Southwell

Nottingham Castle

NORTHAMPTONSHIRE.

Northamptonshire is an inland county, containing 199,000 people. The chief places in it are the city of Peterborough and the town of Northampton.

The North part of the county is very flat, but the other parts are pleasantly varied with hill and dale. Great numbers of cattle are fed here; the sheep are generally of the Leicestershire sort, and the oxen and cows of the short-horned kind. The barley grown in Northamptonshire is fine and abundant, and there is a good quantity of other corn produced. There are also some fine woods.

Peterborough was founded by Penda, the King of Mercia; and it takes its name, which means Peter's town, from St. Peter, to whom the Cathedral was dedicated when it was part of an Abbey of Benedictine Monks. The Cathedral was built in the twelfth and thirteenth centuries. It is a very handsome building, and the situation is a favourable one. Till the time of Charles I., it was kept in a very perfect state, but was much injured during the

NORTHAMPTONSHIRE.

civil wars. Catharine of Aragon, the Queen of Henry VIII., is buried here; but there is no tomb to mark the spot.

Northampton is a pretty town. But little is known of it in very ancient times, but it seems to have been founded before the reign of Alfred; and in the reigns of Richard I., John, and Henry III., it was a place of importance, and contained a mint. The castle at this time was a royal palace, in which some of the scenes of Shakspere's play of King John are laid. In the wars, called the Wars of the Roses, a great battle was fought near the town, in which King Henry VI. was overcome and taken prisoner by Edward IV.

The principal trade of Northampton, Towcester, and several places near them, consists in boots and shoes; and from these towns most of the ready-made shoes sold in London come.

The unfortunate Mary Queen of Scots was tried and beheaded in this county at Fotheringay Castle. Her son James I. ordered the castle to be destroyed when he became King of England, in order that it might not remain as a memorial of the sad event.

Peterborough Cathedral

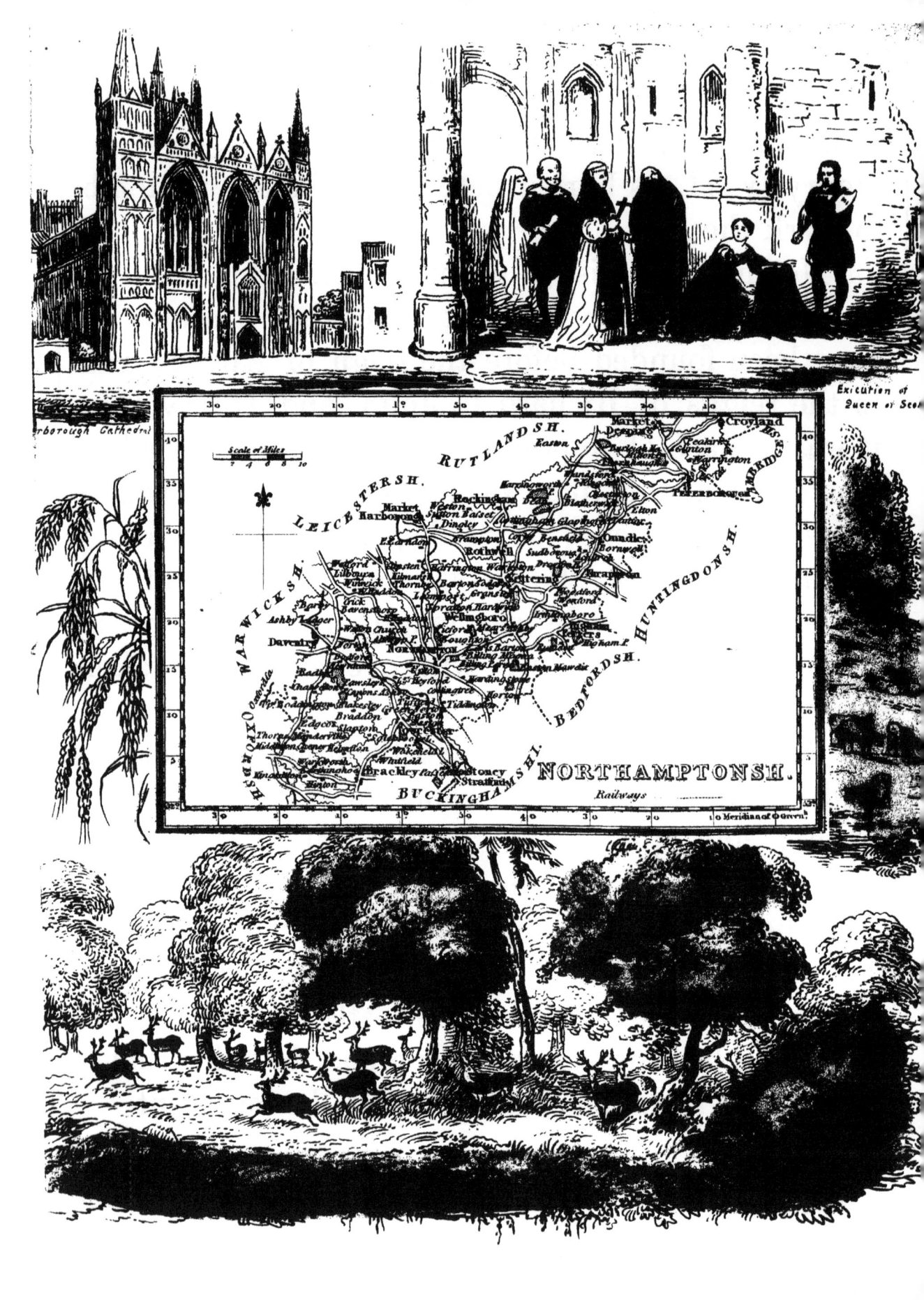

Execution of Queen of Scots

NORTHAMPTONSH.